UNITED NATIONS CONFERENCE ON TRADE AND DEVELOPMENT

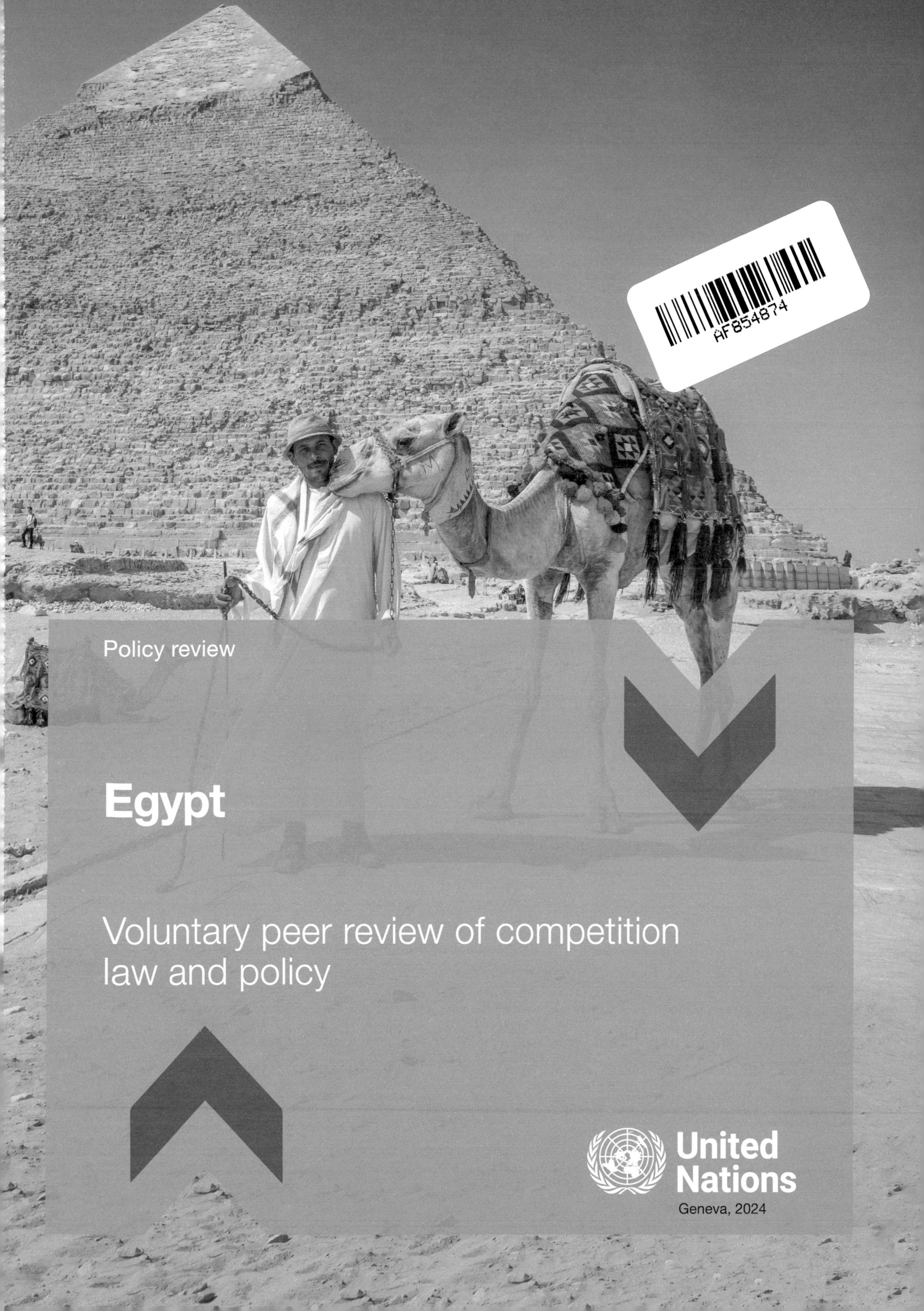

Policy review

Egypt

Voluntary peer review of competition law and policy

United Nations
Geneva, 2024

This publication has been edited externally.

United Nations publication issued by the United Nations
Conference on Trade and Development

UNCTAD/DITC/CLP/2024/1

ISBN: 978-92-1-003165-3
eISBN: 978-92-1-106500-8
Sales No. E.24.II.D.15

Acknowledgements

Voluntary peer reviews of competition law and policy of United Nations Conference on Trade and Development (UNCTAD) are conducted at annual meetings of the Intergovernmental Group of Experts on Competition Law and Policy or at five-yearly United Nations Conference to Review All Aspects of the Set of Multilaterally Agreed Equitable Principles and Rules for the Control of Restrictive Business Practices.

This report was prepared under the guidance of Teresa Moreira, Head of the Competition and Consumer Policies Branch of the UNCTAD Division on International Trade and Development, with Akari Yamamoto-Bonenfant leading on substantive backstopping and review and contribution from Elizabeth Gachuiri, assisted by Yi Zhao, UNCTAD Intern. Magali Studer was responsible for the cover design.

UNCTAD gratefully acknowledges the substantive and insightful contributions of Ioannis Lianos, Professor of Global Competition Law and Policy at the Faculty of Laws, University College London, and Marina Iskander, PhD Candidate, University of Cambridge, and former Head of the Competition Policy and Competitive Neutrality Department, Egyptian Competition Authority, independent experts, on the foundation and history, legal framework and institutional design and recommendations.

UNCTAD expresses appreciation for the enriching assistance of officials of the Egyptian Competition Authority under the leadership of Mahmoud A. Momtaz, Chair, Egyptian Competition Authority, in particular the peer review team led by Toka Hesham, Deputy Head of the International Relations Department, for their valuable comments on the report, as well as for all representatives of public and private sector institutions who were interviewed.

Table of contents

Chapter I

Foundation and history

Over the past few decades, the Egyptian economic system has undergone significant changes, transitioning from protectionism in the 1950s to an open-door policy in the late 1960s. The Egyptian Competition Law (ECL) was eventually enacted in 2005, aiming to regulate economic activities and prevent anti-competitive practices. Subsequent amendments in 2008, 2014, and 2022 introduced merger control regimes, a leniency program, and enhanced the Egyptian Competition Authority (ECA)'s independence. ECL is enforced through a criminal enforcement model with a dual-tier system: ECA makes administrative decisions, while the judiciary imposes fines on cases brought by the public prosecution.

1. Foundation and history

1.1 Purpose of the Voluntary Peer Review of Competition Law and Policy of Egypt

This Voluntary Peer Review Report examines several aspects relating to competition law and policy in Egypt. Specifically, it reviews Law No. 3 of 2005 on the Protection of Competition and the Prohibition of Monopolistic Practices (the Egyptian Competition Law; ECL) and its accompanying Executive Regulations (ECLER) by assessing the substantive aspects of the law relating to the prohibition of anti-competitive behaviour and merger control. It also assesses the Egyptian Competition Authority (ECA) as an institution, namely regarding its independence, powers (including those relating to preventing anti-competitive state measures and promoting competitive neutrality), and case record, as well as its broader competition advocacy role. The Report makes use of documents and data provided by ECA to the authors, or which are otherwise publicly available, relies on desk-based research on legal and economic literature regarding the substantive and procedural rules of ECL, refers to international best practices, and also relies on semi-structured interviews with stakeholders.[1] Building on the analysis undertaken, the Report proposes recommendations to improve the legal and institutional frameworks, as well as the effectiveness of Egypt's competition law and policy.

The remainder of this Introductory Section lays out the legal and economic context of Egyptian competition law and policy and proceeds to describe the main aspects of the law (supported by Annex II).

1.2. Legal and economic context

The Egyptian economic system has, in the past few decades, undergone a number of radical changes. Market policies and the degree of state intervention have changed over the years, most notably from a period of protectionism starting in the 1950s and eventually to an "open-door policy" initiated in the late 1960s.[2]

Throughout this period, competition-related provisions were included in various pieces of legislation. As explained in more detail in Section 3.1.3, Articles 345 and 346 of the Egyptian Penal Code[3] prohibit conspiring between market players for the purposes of increasing prices, hoarding products, or any other "deceitful" actions.[4] The first application of these articles was in 1909, when a district court issued a decision regarding an agreement between a flour mill owner to rent the mills belonging to four other mill owners, in exchange for them discontinuing their production. The court found this practice to be anti-competitive and sentenced the owner to three months of imprisonment (suspended for five years).[5]

1 Interviews were organized with the staff members of the ECA, an official from the Consumer Protection Authority and an official from the Investment Authority, as well as a representative of the main consumer association and a representative of the main business association.

2 Afaf Lutfi Al-Sayyid Marsot, A History of Egypt, Cambridge University Press, 2012, p. 158.

3 The current version of the Penal Code was promulgated in 1937, so it is usually denoted as such, but the first form of the Penal Code dates back to 1904.

4 See Section 3.1.3 for further discussion on imprisonment as a sanction for violations of ECL.

5 Mahmoud A. Momtaz, Revisiting the Imprisonment Sentence under the Egyptian Competition Regime, World Competition, Volume 40, Issue 4, 2017, p. 637-654, 642; and Mahmoud A. Momtaz, The Assessment of Anti-competitive Multifaced Arrangements and the Egyptian Competition Policy (PhD Thesis), Faculty of Law, University of Hamburg, 2018.

In addition, a 1953 court decision further highlights the willingness of the judiciary to prohibit anti-competitive conduct, including those carried out by the state. In this case, an undertaking filed a case to the administrative court, claiming that a group of undertakings had influenced a government authority to issue a decision setting discount margins for all cotton traders. The court found this to be a form of anti-competitive agreement, irrespective of the prohibition under the Penal Code. The court annulled the administrative decision.[6]

Moreover, Law No. 241 of 1959 on the Prevention of Monopoly on the Distribution of Locally Produced Goods prohibited distributors from having a monopoly over locally produced goods that are subject to an import ban.[7]

It was not until the 1990s and early 2000s, however, that Egypt began drafting its own specialized competition statute. This can be traced to the economic reforms and international trade agreements taking place at the time.

In 1991, Egypt implemented an economic reform programme, referred to as the Economic Reform and Structural Adjustment Program, in cooperation with the International Monetary Fund and the World Bank.[8] The need to create a more competitive market, perhaps through the adoption of specialized competition law, became apparent during this time, also following a number of free trade agreements that Egypt had entered into with many countries, which referred to the need for the adoption of adopt rules regulating competition and anti-monopolistic practices.[9]

Moreover, as talks about creating and enacting a competition law matured and were accompanied by a competition enforcement agency, drafts of the consumer law were also discussed.[10] Ideas of creating a joint competition and consumer authority were floated, but ultimately, two separate authorities were created, enabling each to focus on their specific mandate. This is in line with similar institutional practices within the Egyptian state, and it accounted for the high case load which each authority would later face (see Sections 3.2.6 and 3.2.7 for a discussion of ECA's resources and caseload).

As was the case in the 1990s, informal markets still characterize many aspects of the Egyptian economy.[11] Recent data shows that the informal sector accounts for 40 per cent of Egypt's GDP.

6 Mohamed ElFar and Mahmoud A. Momtaz, Challenging Anti-competitive Governmental Decisions under the Egyptian Competition Regime, 36 European Competition Law Review 12, 2015, p. 526-532, 530. Available at: https://papers.ssrn.com/sol3/papers.cfm?abstract_id=2700611.

7 Note also the Order of the Vice Military Governor General No. 5-1973, which criminalized the imposition of a minimum resale price for ration products. Ordinance No. 5-1973 criminalized the refusal to sell a ration product to consumers or to some of them. This order did not only criminalize the unilateral refusal to deal, but also agreements to the same purpose.

8 Ahmed Farouk Ghoneim, Competition Law and Competition Policy: What Does Egypt Really Need?, ERF Working Paper Series, 2002. Available at: https://erf.org.eg/app/uploads/2017/05/0239Ghoneim.pdf.

9 See, for instance, the association agreement with the European Union in 2005 which highlighted the incompatibility of anticompetitive practices with potential foreign trade and investment. Article 72 of that agreement provided incentives for the establishment and implementation of competition legislation. For a discussion, see, for example, K. Attia, Introducing Competition Law and Policy: The case of Egypt, Mediterranean Competition Bulletin, n° 1, October 2009, p. 18; H. Shahein, How is the EU seeking to influence Competition Llaw in Egypt?, Mediterranean Competition Bulletin, n° 6, April 2012, p. 54; and OECD, Competition Law and Policy in Egypt, 2011.

10 Dina I. Waked, Law, Society, and the Market: Living with Egypt's Competition Law 2005-2015, Law and Society in Post-Revolution Egypt (AUC Press) 2018, p. 3. Available at: https://papers.ssrn.com/sol3/papers.cfm?abstract_id=3091552.

11 Maged Ezzeldeen, Shedding light on Egypt's shadow economy. Available at: https://www.pwc.com/m1/en/publications/shedding-light-on-egypts-shadow-economy.html#:~:text=Egypt%20is%20no%20exception.,jobs%20being%20year%2Dround%20occupations; Muhammed Khalid, Egypt's informal economy: Untapped potential that could add $127 bln to GDP. Available at: https://english.ahram.org.eg/News/505338.aspx; OECD, OECD Economic Surveys Egypt. Available at: https://read.oecd-ilibrary.org/economics/oecd-economic-surveys-egypt-2024_af900de2-en#page130; and Nadir Mohammed, Roberta Gatti, Marco Ranzani, Gladys Lopez-Acevedo, Nistha Sinha and Adam Elsheikhi, Informal employment in Egypt, Morocco, & Tunisia: What can we learn to boost inclusive growth? Available at: https://blogs.worldbank.org/en/arabvoices/informal-employment-egypt-morocco-tunisia-what-can-we-learn-boost-inclusive-growth.

Informal employment rates are currently around 60 per cent, with the majority of jobs operating in construction sites, operating vehicles, or street trading.

Eventually, various drafts of ECL were prepared and finally enacted in 2005, as is discussed in Annex II. The constitutional importance of the ECL regime was further strengthened with the 2014 amendments to the Egyptian Constitution, in particular to Article 27:

"The economic system aims at achieving prosperity in the country through sustainable development and social justice to guarantee an increase in the real growth rate of the national economy, raising the standard of living, increasing job opportunities, reducing unemployment rates and eliminating poverty.

The economic system is committed to the criteria of transparency and governance, supporting competitiveness, encouraging investment, achieving balanced growth with regards to geography, sector and the environment; **preventing monopolistic practices**, taking into account the financial and commercial balance and a fair tax system; regulating market mechanisms; guaranteeing different types of ownership; and achieving balance between the interests of different parties to maintain the rights of workers and protect consumers. [...]".[12]

Overall, the Egyptian competitive landscape in the past few years has improved significantly and measurably.[13] For instance, the 2019 Global Competitiveness Report ranks Egypt 100th (out of 141) in the category of "Product Market", which measures the distortive effect of taxes and subsidies on competition, extent of market dominance, and competition in services.[14] This was an improvement compared to Egypt's ranking in the preceding years.[15]

A more recent evaluation was carried out by the United Nations Economic and Social Commission for Western Asia (UN-ESCWA), which conducted a performance evaluation report of the legislative frameworks for the business environment in the Arab region, comparing the situation in 2020 and 2023.[16] The results showed that ECL stood at 4.45 (developed) in 2020, a score that was improved in 2023 and reached 5.73 (strong). Similarly, combating cartels and anti-competitive agreements rose from 5.00 (strong) to 6.13 (very strong). As for competition enforcement practices, the results in 2020 stood at 4.67 (developed) and in 2023 scored 6.36 (very strong). Regarding the merger regulatory regime, in 2020, Egypt achieved 5.83 (strong), and the results improved to 7.00 (very strong) in 2023.

The above data shows that competition in the Egyptian market has seen an improvement over the past few years, which is at least in part attributable to competition law and policy. The strengths and weaknesses of this law, and the institutions enforcing it, are explored further throughout this Report.

1.3. Background: the promulgation of Egyptian Competition Law and its amendments

ECL was promulgated on 15 February 2005, and was to be enacted three months later, on 16 May 2005. The original text set out the aim of ECL in Article 1: that economic activity is carried

12 Emphasis added.

13 It was stated by all interviewees, including the interviewee from the consumer association and the interviewee from the business association, that there has been a significant progress in recent years regarding the role of ECA and the importance of competition law enforcement for business in Egypt.

14 Klaus Schwab, World Economic Forum, The Global Competitiveness Report, 2019, p. 200. Available at: http://www3.weforum.org/docs/WEF_TheGlobalCompetitivenessReport2019.pdf.

15 Egypt ranked 121 of 140 in the 2018 Global Competitiveness Report (Available at: https://www3.weforum.org/docs/GCR2018/05FullReport/TheGlobalCompetitivenessReport2018.pdf), and 112 of 138 in the 2016-2017 Global Competitiveness Report (Available at: https://www3.weforum.org/docs/GCR2016-2017/05FullReport/TheGlobalCompetitivenessReport2016-2017_FINAL.pdf).

16 See https://www.unescwa.org/publications/arab-business-legislative-frameworks-2023.

out in a manner that does not prevent, restrict, or harm competition, in line with the provisions of ECL. The law prohibited certain types of horizontal agreements, anti-competitive vertical restraints, and an exhaustive list of conduct prohibited for undertakings occupying a dominant position. In terms of the institutional powers of ECA, the original version of the law clarified that ECA is affiliated with the "competent minister" and granted the minister key powers, such as referring the cases to the public prosecution and settling with infringers. Article 2 of ECL's preamble clarifies that the competent minister is the Prime Minister. Notably, however, these powers were delegated to the Minister of Trade and Industry shortly after ECA's creation and until 2022.[17] ECL also set out fines for the infringements of its substantive provisions.

Later, the law was amended in 2008 and 2014, adding an *ex-post* merger notification regime and a leniency programme, and making it mandatory for state entities to consult ECA's opinion before issuing state measures relating to competition. Further, the amendments reduced the power of the competent minister, increasing ECA's independence, as well as increased the monetary amounts for fines.

Most recently, in 2022, the law was amended to introduce an *ex-ante* merger control regime, making it mandatory that persons notify ECA of economic concentrations above a certain threshold before these are implemented, and removing the ex-post merger notification regime.

More details on the evolution of ECL are provided in Annex II.

1.4. Current institutional structure and enforcement procedures

Based on the current version of the law, as explained, this Section lays out the current legal procedures pertaining to competition law, and the institutional structure of ECA, regarding anti-trust and merger decisions.

1.4.1. Enforcement procedure for anti-trust cases

An investigation is launched by ECA following a complaint (or a request from a state authority) or *ex-officio*. ECA then starts the investigation, in line with its powers and the powers bestowed upon its officials (see Section 3.2.2). Anti-trust investigations are overseen by the Investigations Department and the Bid-Rigging Department (see Section 3.2.7), which are split into various teams, and which may be supported by the Economic Intelligence Department. The power of the latter is to systematically monitor different sectors of the economy, mainly through procuring and analysing data (see Section 3.2.3). Figure 1 illustrates the current organizational staff chart at ECA.

According to Article 39 of ECLER, once the case team finalizes its investigation, a report is drafted. As is shown in Figure 1, reports are reviewed by the Technical Office, which is currently staffed with legal and economic consultants to the Chairperson.

[17] This delegation was repealed in August 2022 through Prime Ministerial Decision No. 2934 of 2022. The issue of ECA's independence is discussed further in Section 3.2.1.

Figure 1
ECA's Organizational Structure (2024)[18]

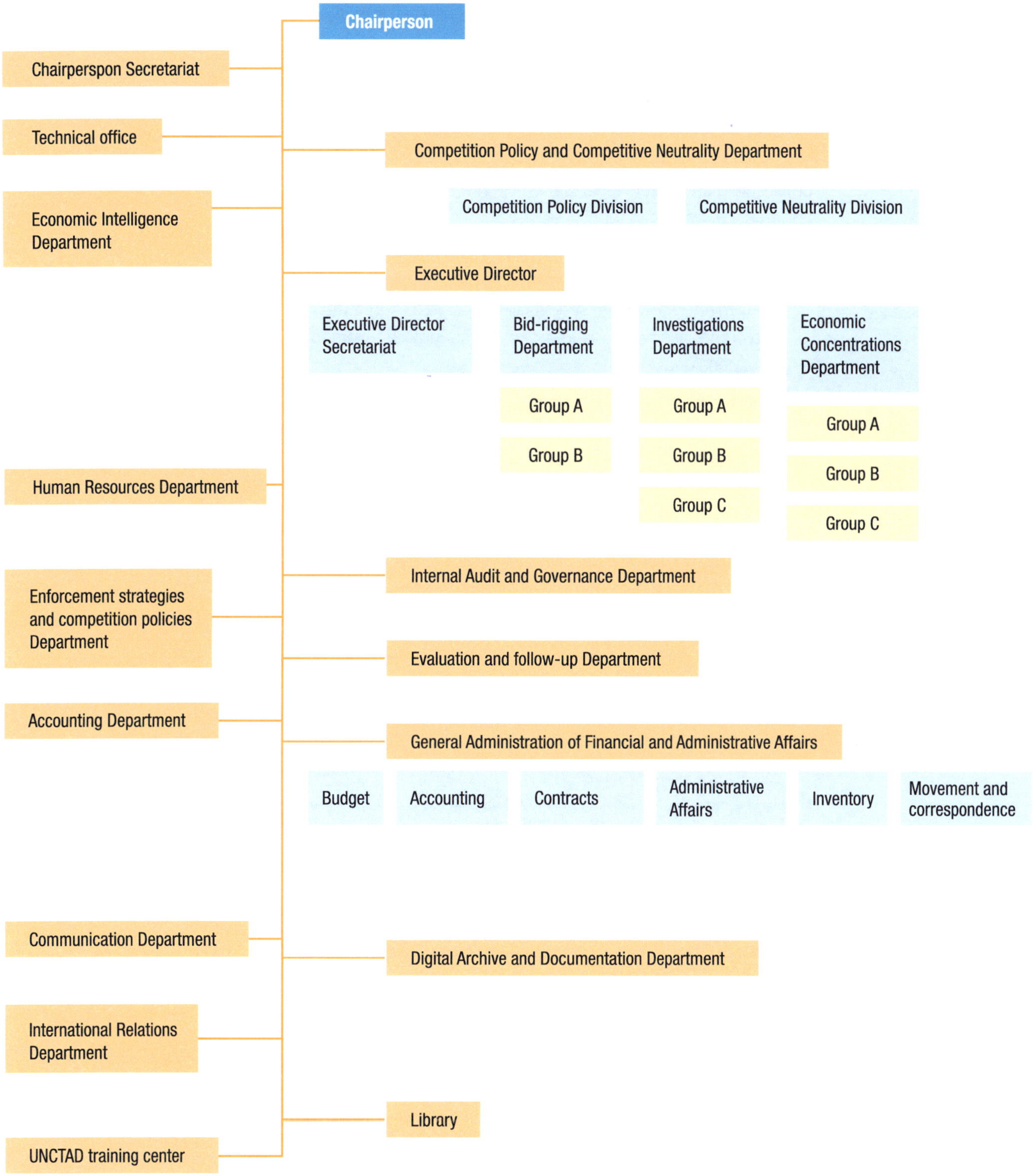

[18] Data obtained from ECA.

The report is then presented to ECA's Board, which can decide whether they agree with the findings of the team or that further investigation is required.[19] The infringing party is then notified, in writing, of ECA's decision.[20] According to Article 13 of ECL, the Board convenes at least once a month, and more often, if necessary, upon the invitation of the Chairperson.

While the violations of ECL are criminal in nature and are described as such throughout the law, the penalties issued by the Economic Courts, are in the form of criminal fines,[21] regardless that the nature of ECA's decisions are administrative. Administrative decisions can be defined, according to Egyptian case law, as: "a unilateral legal act issued by the willingness of an administrative authority of the state, and which creates legal effects, creating a new legal stance or amending or repealing an existing legal stance".[22] The enforcement decisions that ECA can undertake for anti-trust cases are:

(1) Interim measures: according to paragraph 2 of Article 20 of ECL, ECA's Board can issue a decision to suspend practices before it terminates its investigation, if these practices appear preliminarily to violate Articles 6 to 8 of ECL and if they seem to cause substantial harm to competition or consumers which cannot be reversed in the absence of the temporary suspension.

(2) Infringement decisions, including decisions to adopt behavioural and/or structural remedies on the infringers in order to restore the competition in the affected market(s): According to paragraph 1 of Article 20 of ECL, once ECA establishes a violation of Articles 6 to 8 of ECL, it must order the infringing parties to redress the violation or to undertake corrective measures (behavioural and/or structural remedies), either immediately or within a set period of time. If the anti-competitive agreement or contract is not terminated within this time, it is considered null and void.[23] Furthermore, ECA can, according to paragraph 1 of Article 21 of ECL, choose to send a request to the public prosecution to initiate criminal proceedings.[24]

(3) Up until a final judgment is made by the highest court, ECA can accept a request for settlement with the infringers and accordingly issue a decision determining the settlement amount (see Section 3.1.1 for further discussion on settlements).

Since these decisions are administrative decisions, they are governed by the State Council Law

[19] Article 40 of ECLER.

[20] Article 43 of ECLER. Note that this notification is through a letter containing the final decision of the Board; i.e. the provisions of ECL infringed, the cease-and-desist order, and a notification that a referral has been sent to the public prosecution or that the settlement request has been accepted (whichever applies, if either). Currently, there is no legal obligation, nor is there an internal mechanism at ECA, to send a copy of the report to the infringing parties. They may, at the discretion of ECA, be sent a non-confidential version of the report if they show willingness to settle with ECA.

[21] Specifically, they are considered "misdemeanours" rather than "crimes", as per Article 11 of the Penal Code, which define misdemeanours as violations with a penalty of over EGP 100 and crimes as those with imprisonment or death sentences (Article 10).

[22] Mohamed Fouad Mehanna, Administrative Decisions in the Administrative Laws of Egypt and France, The Law Journal for Legal and Economic Research (University of Alexandria), Issue 3.4, 1958, p. 1-84. Available (in Arabic) at: https://lalexu.journals.ekb.eg/article_299159_33aa34915db7a3ff429949bfc4eaa661.pdf.

[23] It is interesting to note here that ECA's power to adopt cease-and-desist orders, as well as to order the violator to readjust their situation and to redress the violation or to undertake corrective measures could be interpreted as involving behavioural or structural remedies that not only bring an end to the infringement, but also redress to the situation. Note that there is not specific preference expressed for behavioural remedies as is provided for in Article 7 of Regulation 1/2003, which empowers the European Commission to impose on the infringing undertakings any behavioural or structural remedies which are proportionate to the infringement committed and necessary to bring the infringement effectively to an end but also stipulates that "[s]tructural remedies can only be imposed either where there is no equally effective behavioural remedy or where any equally effective behavioural remedy would be more burdensome for the undertaking concerned than the structural remedy. [...]". For a discussion of discretionary remedialism in competition law see, I. Lianos, Competition Law Remedies in Europe, in I. Lianos & D. Geradin (eds.), Handbook on European Competition Law (Edward Elgar, 2013), p. 362-455.

[24] This is considered a request by ECA and not an administrative decision.

No. 47 of 1972 (SCL), which becomes relevant when it comes to appeal procedures. According to Article 24 of SCL, a grievance of a decision issued by ECA can be submitted to ECA within 60 days of informing the party addressed by the decision. ECA must then respond to the grievance within 60 days of receiving it, and the absence of a response equates to rejecting the grievance. The party addressed by the decision can then raise the matter to the administrative courts within 60 days of receiving a response, or after the first 60-day period has ended. The administrative courts assess the decision in terms of procedure and substance.[25] [26]

As mentioned above, ECA can request that the public prosecution initiate criminal proceedings for a particular infringement. According to Article 21 of ECL, the public prosecution cannot initiate criminal proceedings relating to the provisions of ECL without a written request from ECA. The branch of the public prosecution dealing with ECL violations is the Economic Affairs and Money Laundering Division.[27]

While ECA is the only entity that may request to initiate criminal procedures, Article 1 of the Law on Criminal Procedures (No. 150 of 1950) (LCP) sets out that the public prosecution is the only entity with the power to file a criminal case at the court. Accordingly, the power to file a case does not belong to ECA, but rather to the public prosecution. This is done as follows:

Once the public prosecution receives an initial request from ECA, it begins to investigate the case. Notably, the evidence gathered by ECA and referred to the prosecution is carried out by its law enforcement officers,[28] who have the power to "inquire, inspect, and collect information,"[29] similar to the powers of police officers. The public prosecution, on the other hand, is the only entity with a stronger power of "investigation".[30] In the course of its investigation, the public prosecution will review the evidence received from ECA.[31] It can also call upon the investigation team at ECA as a witness. Additionally, the prosecution may decide that additional evidence is required. The public prosecution can procure this evidence through its own officers, or, according to Article 200 of LCP, through "any law enforcement officer it bequests" within the realm of the officer's powers. This means that the public prosecution can appoint one or more officials at ECA to carry out further investigations. However, in that case, the ECA officials would be carrying out work on behalf of the public prosecution and not ECA, meaning that they would report to the former and not the latter.

Based on the evidence gathered initially by ECA or by further investigations, either directly by the public prosecution or by other law enforcement officers, the public prosecution has the following options:

(1) If it finds that there is no reason to proceed in the case, it can terminate procedures (Article 61 of LCP). The prosecution can reach this conclusion after it has exerted efforts to gather all the evidence related to the case but has come to the conclusion that the evidence does not point to the occurrence of the crime or that it is adequately unlikely that the defendant will be found guilty by the court.[32]

---

25 Article 10 of SCL.

26 Notably, since 2015, six appeals of infringement decisions have been launched at the Administrative Courts, and none have been successful. As of the time of the writing of this publication, four are still ongoing.

27 This Division was created by a Decision of the Minister of Justice dated 23 October 1985. After the promulgation of Law No. 120 of 2008, Creating the Economic Courts (discussed further below), Circular No. 26 of 2008 clarified that this Division would be responsible for investigating crimes under the jurisdiction of the Economic Courts, which include the crimes listed in ECL. The Division was previously named the Financial and Economic Affairs Division, but it was renamed following the issue of Law No. 154 of 2022, Amending Some Provisions of the Money Laundering Law, which placed money laundering cases under its jurisdiction.

28 As explained in Section 3.2.2, lawyers, economists, and information technology specialists at ECA hold the status of law enforcement officers.

29 Article 11 of ECL.

30 Article 1 of LCP.

31 Article 776 of the General Instructions for Prosecution Offices.

32 Article 803 of General Instructions for Prosecution Offices.

(2) If it finds that there is enough evidence to file a case, it can request that the defendant appear before the competent court (Article 63 of LCP). Again, only the public prosecution can make the decision to file a case.

Accordingly, although ECA has the power to request the initiation of criminal proceedings, it has no control over whether or not the case is brought to the courts. Cases referred to the public prosecution are ultimately investigated by officials at the Economic Affairs and Money Laundering Division, who, although experienced in legal affairs, are not necessarily experienced in ECL. Their jurisdiction covers various other laws such as those relating to banks, financial institutions, and money-laundering. As such, there can be practices that ECA has investigated, following complaint, request, or ex-officio, and has accordingly found to infringe ECL, which go unpunished because ECA does not have fining powers (see Section 3.1.2) and the public prosecution has decided not to pursue them. According to the figures provided by ECA, seven (7) out of the fifteen (15) cases referred to the public prosecution since the creation of ECA have not been followed through for criminal prosecution by the public prosecution, although this does not necessarily mean that the violation has not been substantiated in these cases. Furthermore, this may duplicate investigative resources elongating procedures for the imposition of fines for anticompetitive conduct. One way to resolve this issue is to create an amendment in ECL in order to provide ECA the additional power to request that a case is *filed* rather than the more limited power of requesting that criminal procedures are initiated. While it would still ultimately be at the discretion of the public prosecution to file the case, this would involve ECA in the investigative process of the prosecution, as the prosecutor would have to revert to ECA before filing a case. This would enable ECA to benefit from the prosecution's higher investigation powers, as well as allow the prosecutor to benefit more concretely from ECA's experience, before filing a case.

If the public prosecution decides to proceed, the case is brought in front of the Economic Courts. The Economic Courts have competence over the application of several laws concerning economic and commercial affairs, such as banking law, financial regulations, consumer protection, telecommunications, investment, and intellectual property.[33] They are organized into two levels: the Court of First Instance and the Court of Appeal.[34] The Economic Courts can, at both levels, request the opinion of experts in competition law who are registered at the Ministry of Justice.[35] Decisions of the Economic Court of Appeal can be challenged in front of the State's Court of Cassation,[36] which shall address the substantive aspects of the case.[37] Note here that any decision by the court is issued against individuals rather than undertakings (which may nevertheless be jointly liable); Article 25 of ECL lays out that "[t]he person responsible for the actual management of the undertaking in violation shall be subject to the same penalties prescribed for the acts committed in violation of the provisions of this Law, if it has been proven that such person had actual knowledge of such violation and that his failure to perform the obligations imposed on him by reason of the management contributed to the violation. The undertaking shall be jointly liable for the payment of the fines and compensation ruled, if the violation has been committed by one of its employees, acting in the name or on behalf of the undertaking".

Accordingly, ECL is enforced through a criminal enforcement model. There is a dual/two-tier institutional regime, according to which ECA may take administrative decisions while the judiciary may also decide the imposition of fines to the cases brought before it by the public prosecution. Note that the appeal process is different for each of these systems. This model is summarized in Figure 2:

33 Article 4 of Law No. 120 of 2008 Creating the Economic Courts.
34 Article 1 of Law No. 120 of 2008 Creating the Economic Courts.
35 Article 9 of Law No. 120 of 2008 Creating the Economic Courts.
36 Articles 11 and 12 of Law No. 120 of 2008 Creating the Economic Courts.
37 Article 12 of Law No. 120 of 2008 Creating the Economic Courts.

Figure 2

Enforcement Procedures for Anti-Trust Cases[38]

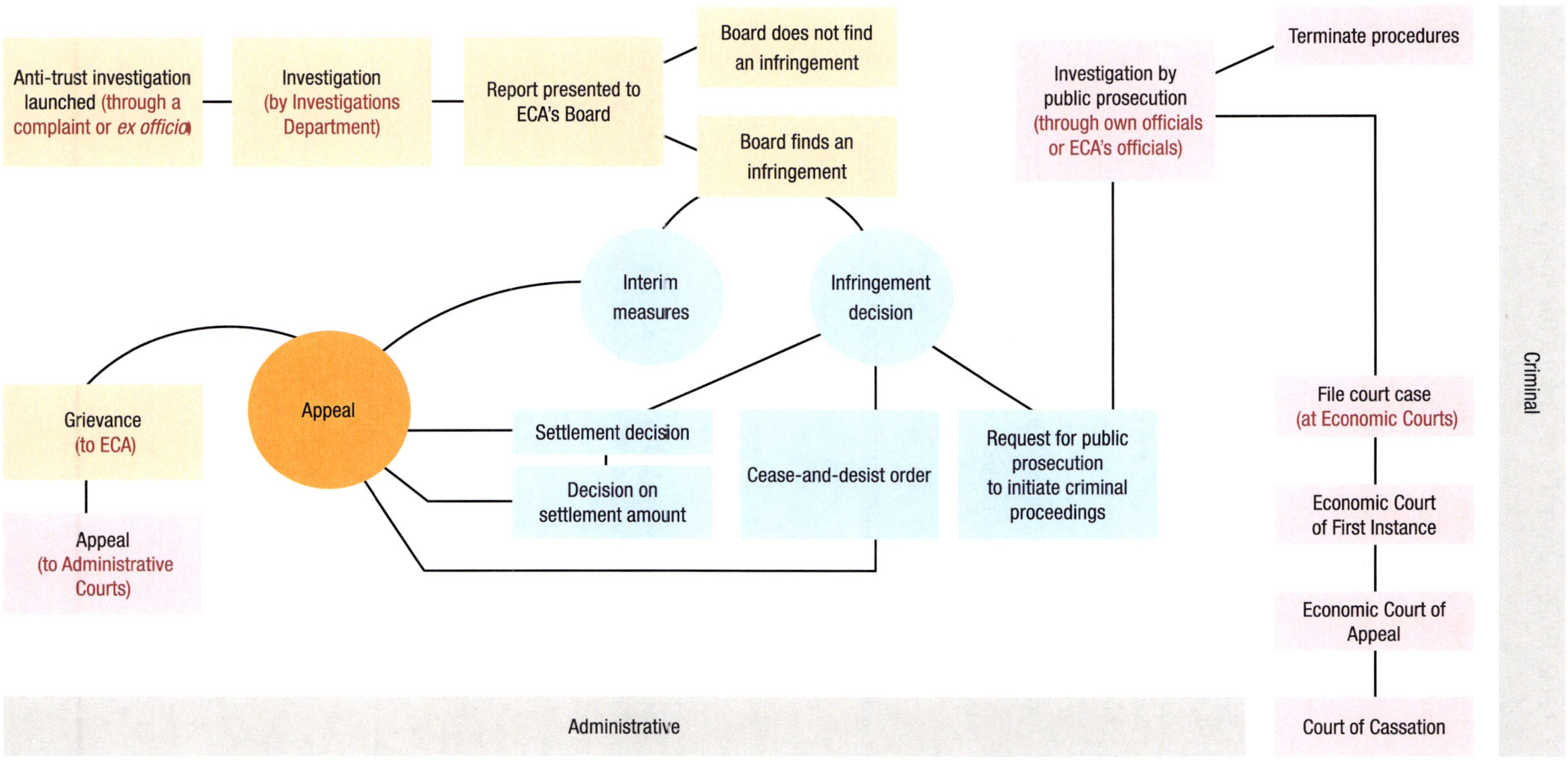

[38] Prepared by the authors based on provisions of ECL and ECLER and data obtained from ECA.

1.4.2. Enforcement procedure for merger cases

The procedures for merger cases are not yet as clear as those for anti-trust cases, as ECLER has not been amended to reflect the new *ex-ante* merger control regime. However, it is apparent from Figure 1 above that there is a dedicated Economic Concentrations Department at ECA. The Department currently works on creating material and guidance for when the law is implemented, and it deals with notifications received from the Common Market for Eastern and Southern Africa (COMESA) Competition Commission and from the sector regulators in the healthcare sector (see Section 2.1.4).

Moreover, according to the newly added provisions of ECL, the decisions relating to merger control are administrative in nature. Decisions are issued by committees, created in line with Article 27 of ECLER,[39] composed of three Board members, for Phase I decisions[40] and for cases referred from FRA,[41] and by ECA's Board for Phase II decisions[42] (see Annex A.1.5. for the timelines and possible outcomes of each stage). As these decisions are administrative, their mechanism of appeal is as described in Section 1.4.1.

In addition, ECA's Board can refer certain infringements relating to merger control (laid out in Article 19 bis d of ECL) to the public prosecution for criminal prosecution:

(1) Failure to notify a notifiable transaction.

(2) Gun jumping (implementing the transaction before ECA has issued a decision, ignoring the stand-still obligation laid out in Article 19 bis a of ECL).

(3) The breach of the conditions upon which a conditional clearance of an economic concentration is issued.

(4) Failure to comply with a blocking decision.

(5) Obtaining a clearance decision from ECA or Financial Regulatory Authority (FRA) based on misleading data, information, and/or documents, which were knowingly submitted to ECA.

As with the mechanism for anti-trust cases, ECA's power is limited to requesting the initiation of criminal proceedings; it cannot directly file the case at the court.

[39] Article 27 of ECLER notes "[t]he Board of Directors may assign one of its members or a committee formed among them to carry out a specific assignment or to supervise a certain aspect of the Authority's activities. In such cases, reports on the assignment or supervision shall be prepared and presented to the Board".

[40] Article 19 bis c of ECL.

[41] Article 19 bis f of ECL.

[42] Article 19 bis d of ECL.

Chapter II

Legal framework

ECL prohibits certain horizontal agreements, anti-competitive vertical agreements, abuse of dominant position, and economic concentrations that substantially restrict, lessen, or harm the freedom of competition. However, several issues have emerged from this legal framework, and it does not adequately cover exploitative abuses or digital market issues. Debate also arises from competition jurisdiction in the telecommunications sector, stemming from the anti-trust and merger control powers of the Central Bank of Egypt (CBE) and the Financial Regulatory Authority (FRA). This necessitates a comparison to international best practices, which could offer useful recommendations for reformation.

2. Legal framework

2.1. Egyptian Competition Law: assessment of the clarity, coherence, and effectiveness of the legal framework

As discussed in Section 1 and Annex II, ECL was promulgated in 2005 and has been amended since. In its current form, ECL prohibits certain horizontal agreements, anti-competitive vertical agreements, abuse of dominant position, and economic concentrations that substantially restrict, lessen, or harm the freedom of competition. Sector-specific regulators also play a role in this framework. This Section will explore the substance of each of these prohibitions, as well as the role of sector specific regulators, concluding with a comparison to the substance of competition laws and policies of other jurisdictions.

2.1.1. Horizontal agreements

As previously outlined, Article 6 of ECL, and Article 11 of ECLER, prohibit four types of agreements between competitors. It also lays out a mechanism for the *ex-ante* exemption of horizontal agreements that will result in economic efficiencies, which outweigh the harm to competition and are passed on to consumers.

Article 6 of ECL:

"Any agreement or contract between competing persons in any relevant market is prohibited if they are intended to result in any of the following:

a) Increasing, decreasing, or fixing prices of sale or purchase of products subject matter of dealings.
b) Dividing markets or allocating them based on geographic areas, distribution centres, customer types, goods, market shares, seasons, or time periods.
c) Coordinating regarding proceeding or refraining from participating in tenders, auctions, negotiations and other calls for procurement.
d) Restricting the manufacturing, production, distribution, or marketing operations for products, including restricting the type, size, characteristics, or availability of the product.

[...]"

Article 11 of ECLER:

"Agreements or contracts between competing persons in any relevant market shall be prohibited if they are intended to result in any of the following:

a) Increasing, decreasing or fixing prices of sale or purchase of products subject matter of dealings. Determination of price shall cover due returns on instalments, warranty duration, after sale services and any other contractual conditions that influence the purchasing or selling decision.
b) Dividing markets or allocating them based on geographic areas, distribution centres, customer types, goods, market shares, seasons or time periods.

c) Coordinating regarding proceeding or refraining from participating in tenders, auctions, negotiations and other calls for procurement. The indications that are taken into consideration for the existence of such coordination are, in particular, the following:

1- Submitting identical bids, including agreeing on common rules for calculating prices or determining tender conditions.

2- Agreement on the person who will submit the bid, including the prior agreement on the person who will be awarded the bid whether through rotation, geographical basis or customer division basis.

3- Agreement on submitting fictitious bids.

4- Agreement to prevent a person from submitting or participating in bid submissions.

d) Restricting the manufacturing, production, distribution or marketing operations for products, including restricting the type, size, characteristics or availability of the product.

[...]"

Box 1 below shows cases where ECA found violations of Article 6 of ECL.

Box 1
Selected Article 6 Cases

Article 6(a): In 2023, ECA found that representative offices of two publishing houses, in cooperation with their authorised distributors, had engaged in anticompetitive agreements aimed to increase the prices of educational books that are exported from abroad by agreeing upon an exchange rate that exceeded the official exchange rate of the Central Bank of Egypt by 80 per cent, in violation of Article 6 (a) of ECL. Additionally, they engaged in market allocation agreements by dividing schools among authorised distributors in violation of Article 6 (b) of ECL. The anti-competitive agreements resulted in increasing financial burdens on Egyptian families and limiting schools' choices, in addition to creating barriers to entry for distributors aiming to enter the market. The parties eventually settled with ECA.[43] In 2022, ECA found a number of egg brokers to have agreed on the price of the egg carton daily. It proved the violation and referred it to the public prosecution.[44] In 2019, ECA received a complaint that two undertakings in the market for laser hair removal had agreed to set the prices for their services. Through its investigation, ECA uncovered that 21 undertakings had agreed, via a group on the instant messaging platform WhatsApp, to set a minimum price for their services. ECA also met with all members of the cartel and obtained written testimonies from them. Accordingly, it issued an infringement decision in 2021, and the parties settled with ECA.[45]

Article 6(b): In 2011, ECA received a complaint that two undertakings in the market for starch had been agreed for the express purpose of dividing and identifying consumers among them by the type of consumer. ECA analysed the market in question and found that the presence of high barriers to entry, as well as the close relationship

[43] ECA, Infringement of Publishers of School Books, 25 February 2023. Available (in Arabic) here.
[44] ECA, ECA Refers Egg Brokers to Public Prosecution, 28 July 2022. Available (in Arabic) here.
[45] ECA, Annual Report on Competition Policy Developments in Egypt 2021, p. 7. Available at: https://one.oecd.org/document/DAF/COMP/AR(2022)44/en/pdf.

between the two undertakings in question, made the agreement likely. It also obtained direct evidence of the agreement in the form of testimonies from the CEOs of the undertakings. ECA issued an infringement decision in 2013 and referred the case to the public prosecution.[46]

Article 6(c): In 2023, ECA launched an initiation and subsequently issued an infringement decision against two undertakings which had committed bid-rigging regarding procurement contracts with the Cairo Transport Authority. ECA also informed the authority of the practices, as well as took the necessary steps to debar them from entering into future contracts with the State (see Section 3.1.3).[47] Also in 2023, ECA issued a decision against 33 printing companies for agreeing on a minimum bid to be presented to the Ministry of Education.[48] ECA also proved two separate violations, following *ex officio* investigations, by ten undertakings operating in the market for lamp posts (2022), which offered identical price offers and divided the quantities among them with some of the tenders, and five in the market for iron pipes (2023), both were in regard to contracts with the state.[49]

Article 6(d): In 2018, ECA received a complaint that two undertakings, which produced and sold two types of medication to treat Virus C, had agreed to only sell these medications in a bundle. This harmed the ability of undertakings that sold only one type of medication to compete on the market (around 20 undertakings). ECA was able to uncover written evidence of the agreement, in the form of e-mail correspondences between the two companies. Therefore, a cease-and-desist order was issued in 2019, and the undertakings were eventually settled with ECA.[50]

The wording of Article 6 of ECL and Article 11 of ECLER, as they prohibit conduct that "intends to" result in the four types of effects listed in the articles, show that Article 6 violations can be found without requiring proof of effects. Accordingly, Article 6 of ECL provides an exhaustive list of horizontal conduct that is prohibited *per se*. Previous court judgments also show this and explain that the concept of agreement is more broadly defined than that of contract: a 2008 court decision states that "[t]he crime of monopolistic agreements, specifically, does not require a certain form, but it is enough for its occurrence that the will of the suspected infringers is met and that they concur to the substance of the agreement".[51]

Also, the term "intends to" refers to agreements and/or contracts that potentially result in one of the effects listed in the exhaustive list set in Article 6 of ECL.

However, the list does not include information exchange as a stand-alone violation. It is recommended that this should be added to Article 6 of ECL.

46 ECA, Annual Report 2013-2014, p. 20. Available (in Arabic) at: http://eca.gov.eg/ECA/upload/Publication/Attachment_A/91/11.pdf.

47 ECA, As a Part of it's Goal to Prosecute Bid-Rigging in Public Procurement… ECA Proves Violation of Two Providers of Spare Parts to the Cairo Transport Authority, 21 May 2023. Available (in Arabic) here.

48 ECA, ECA Proves the Violation of 33 Printing Companies Regarding Printing and Providing Books to the Ministry of Education, 4 January 2024. Available (in Arabic) here.

49 ECA, As a Part of it's Goal to Prosecute Bid-Rigging in Public Procurement… ECA Proves Violation Companies in the Markets for Lamp Posts and Iron Pipes, 30 January 2023. Available (in Arabic) here.

50 ECA, Annual Report 2019-2020, p. 23. Available (in Arabic) at: https://eca.org.eg/getattachment/8d27be44-b787-4040-b93c-a716c598cd7c/%D8%A7%D9%84%D8%AA%D9%82%D8%B1%D9%8A%D8%B1-%D8%A7%D9%84%D8%B3%D9%86%D9%88%D9%8A-2019-2020.pdf.

51 North Cairo Preliminary Court, Case No. 2900 of 2008 for Nasr City.

This is particularly important in the context of digital markets, such as in cases of algorithmic collusion. In such a case, undertakings may employ uniform prices not as a result of a decision to set prices, but as a result of the programming of their algorithms to do so, eventually as a result of an agreement to coordinate algorithms.

Another aspect which is open to interpretation is the meaning of the terms "contract or agreement". Article 11 of ECLER, as well as the literature[52] and case law show that this term is to be interpreted widely to include at least oral and non-binding agreements; for instance, a 2016 court case[53] highlights that the contracts or agreements referred to in Article 6 of ECL are to cover any "meeting of minds". However, in practice, this is more difficult to interpret and implement. This results in less legal certainty as to whether these terms cover (or not) decisions by associations of undertakings and concerted practices as Article 101 of the Treaty on the Functioning of the European Union (TFEU) does under the European Union competition law.[54]

By way of example, this may present a problem when investigating anti-competitive behaviour of members of a trade union. In a hypothetical scenario, a trade union may issue a decision - in the name of its members, who are competitors - which violates Article 6 of ECL, perhaps by restricting the distribution of a certain product for a certain time period. Competitors are all present in the meeting in which the decision was taken, but there is no actual evidence - such as a recording of the meeting - substantiating an explicit agreement between each of the members. Moreover, while the court has previously held that circumstantial evidence of collusion may be accepted,[55] evidence of increased prices following such a meeting, for instance, would still not be sufficient to substantiate that the competitors participated in the cartel. While under European Union case law this may be considered a decision by an association of undertakings, but it would be difficult to substantiate a violation of Article 6 of ECL, although the decision of the association of undertakings leads to a restriction of competition.[56]

52 Established literature on the Egyptian legal system clarifies that all contracts encompass agreements, but not all agreements take the form of a contract, meaning that the agreement is a concept wider than that of the contract. See Abdel Razek El Sanhouri, Egyptian Civil Law, 1964, p. 117.

53 Cairo Economic Court, Court of First Instance, Case No. 1898 of 2016.

54 For the European Union competition law to apply to an "association of undertakings" as a separate entity than its members, two elements must be present: (1) the organizational element as the association should have some "lasting corporate structure", although it is irrelevant if the association has legal personality or it is a profit-making organization, and (2) the functional element, which indicates that the association's activities either are of an economic nature, or its members' activities are of an economic nature, that it is indeed an association of 'undertakings. However, if the association is not aware of the illegal conduct of its members, it should not be held liable and the illegal activity in question does not form a decision of an association of undertakings. More generally, see Case C-382/12 P, MasterCard and Others v Commission, ECLI:EU:C:2014:2201.

55 North Cairo Court of First Instance, Case No. 2900 of 2008.

56 This results from a narrow definition of the concept of agreement by ECA in the Cinema case in which the members of the relevant business association held two meetings. The first did not have an anti-competitive purpose, while the second resulted in a decision implying a restriction of competition. In its decision, ECA did not find that the first meeting constituted an infringement, not because of the absence of a restriction of competition, but because the decision of this meeting was formal. Conversely, it found that the decision of the second meeting was an infringement and considered it as an agreement, not by assimilating the association decision to an agreement, but because the decision was taken outside the premises of the association. However, in the subsequent Poultry, the Car Insurance, and Pharmaceutical Products II cases (ECA, Decision on the study of the poultry sector in Egypt, April 16, 2013; ECA, Decision relating to complaints from a citizen and the Consumer Protection Authority against the Royal Insurance Company and the Contact Car Company, April 22, 2014; and ECA, Decision relating to the complaint by the Pharmacists' Union against the companies of the League of Medicines Distributors and Importers, 1 December 2015), ECA considered the association's decisions as agreements between members, although in these cases they were formal decisions following meetings held at the headquarters of the business associations. For a discussion, see F. El-Zahraa Adel, L'effectivité du droit égyptien de la concurrence - Essais de mise en perspective (Thèse de doctorat, Université Paris 1 Panthéon Sorbonne, 2019), p. 52 (arguing that in view of this jurisprudence, there is no need to adopt a separate concept of "decision of association of undertakings" but for ECA to issue guidelines expanding the concept of agreement).

The interpretation of Article 6 of ECL as requiring the definition of the relevant market in order to establish the competitive relationship between the parties to the agreement or contract may also raise concerns. While this provision prohibits agreements or contracts between "competing persons in any relevant market", the wording of Article 11 of ECLER, which clarifies that "competing persons refer to those working in the same relevant market at present or those capable of working in it in the future", may be interpreted as not requiring the relevant market to be defined and delineated for the purposes of an Article 6 case, to the extent that it does not refer to existing competitors but also to potential competitors without however setting some limit as to the immediacy of that potential entry in the specific market.[57] Hence, it should suffice to prove that the undertakings operate in the same market or are capable of working in it in the future, without exploring the precise limits of that market, through for instance, a hypothetical monopolist or Small but significant and non-transitory increase in price (SSNIP) test. This understanding seems to be supported by some decisions of ECA, including in the starch case,[58] three poultry cases,[59] and a more recent "laser" case60 (see Box 1). However, ECA has also thoroughly defined the market in a number of recent cases, such as those relating to conduct by the printing companies, book publishers, iron pipes, and lamp posts (see Box 1), perhaps to ensure that the market and its dynamics are adequately understood throughout the investigation, or to prevent any issues if the case were to be appealed. Note, however, that both the administrative[61] and criminal courts[62] have issued decisions supporting the practice of not defining the market for Article 6 cases. Therefore, to avoid unnecessary burdens on ECA and to promote clarity, Article 6 of ECL should perhaps be amended to delete any reference to the concept of relevant market or to make it clearer that there is no need to proceed to a full-fledged market definition but eventually to sketch the competitive relationship (or not) between the parties to the agreement.[63]

Furthermore, regarding the exemption mechanism laid out in Article 6(2) of ECL, reference is made to Article 2(e) of ECL, which defines economic efficiencies as those that result in "the reduction of the average variable cost of producing goods, the enhancement of quality, or optimizing the volume of goods produced or its distribution or the production or distribution of novel goods or the acceleration of its production or distribution".

57 See European Commission Market Definition Notice (2024), paragraph 23 (noting the importance of the criteria of effectiveness and immediacy of supply-side substitution so as for a competitive constraint to be included in the definition of the market).

58 Starch case (2011).

59 F. El-Zahraa Adel, L'effectivité du droit égyptien de la concurrence - Essais de mise en perspective (Thèse de doctorat, Université Paris 1 Panthéon Sorbonne, 2019).

60 Laser case (2021).

61 Egypt, State Council, Case No. 74232 of judicial year 62.

62 Economic Court of Appeal, Case No. 447 of 2018.

63 F. El-Zahraa Adel, L'effectivité du droit égyptien de la concurrence- Essais de mise en perspective (Thèse de doctorat, Université Paris 1 Panthéon Sorbonne, 2019), p. 77.

This could be interpreted as also covering (industrial) restructuring agreements ("crisis cartels").[64]

For these reasons, Article 6 of ECL should be amended to explicitly expand its current scope on contracts and agreements. It should also be made clear that other types of horizontal agreements which may not be listed as hardcore restrictions are covered by Article 6 but should be subject to an effects analysis or keep Article 6 of ECL for hardcore horizontal restrictions, and all other horizontal or vertical agreements being covered by Article 7 of ECL. Accordingly, the conduct currently listed in Article 6 of ECL could either be kept as such (with the addition of the exchange of information as a stand-alone hardcore restriction), a paragraph being added providing for an effects analysis of any other agreement/collusion between competitors and the exemption mechanism listed in the final paragraph of the article retained. Otherwise, Article 6 of ECL should focus on hardcore restrictions with Article 7 of ECL, as discussed in the following Section, being amended to include a clause prohibiting any other agreements (horizontal or vertical) that have the effect of harming competition.[65] In both cases, the reference to the "relevant market", where it is related to horizontal agreements, should be removed.

64 See OECD, Crisis Cartels - Policy Roundtables, 2011. Available at: https://www.oecd.org/daf/competition/cartels/48948847.pdf. The European Commission has accepted in certain limited circumstances that industrial restructuring agreements ("crisis cartels") which aim to reduce industry overcapacity may justified, in case of course they satisfy the four conditions of Article 101(3) of TFEU. See, for example, Synthetic Fibres (Case IV/30.810) Commission Decision (1984) OJ L 207/17, paragraph 39; Stichting Baksteen (Dutch Bricks) (Case IV/34.456) Commission Decision (1994) OJ L 131/15, paragraphs 26 and 29. One may nevertheless note that the "crisis cartel" is not an exemption/justification of a restriction of competition but a break in the causal link that exists between the specific conduct (restructuring agreement) and the restriction of competition to the extent that this might have happened anyway if the "failing" firms would have in any case exited the market. See for a similar interpretation the "failing firm defence" in the European Union merger control which provides for the possibility under certain conditions of restructuring through consolidation of undertakings following a counterfactual analysis in order to assess whether the competitive structure of the market would deteriorate to a lesser extent if the concentration did not proceed: Joined Cases C-68/94 & C-30/95, French Republic and Société commerciale des potasses et de l'azote (SCPA) and Entreprise minière et chimique (EMC) v Commission of the European Communities (1998) ECR I-1375.

65 See Section 4.1. for a more detailed explanation of this proposal. Note that a similar proposal (Article 6 bis of ECL) was presented in the drafts of the 2014 law amendments, but it was eventually abandoned. This provision would have prohibited agreements whose purpose is to achieve economic efficiency, but which will result in the restriction of competition, unless their pro-competitive effects outweigh their anti-competitive effects. Reading the two provisions together, the distinction between the two categories of agreements would have become clearer: Article 6 of ECL would have referred to hardcore agreements and other restrictions by-object, while Article 6 bis of ECL would have referred to restrictions by-effect. See F. El-Zahraa Adel, L'effectivité du droit égyptien de la concurrence - Essais de mise en perspective (Thèse de doctorat, Université Paris 1 Panthéon Sorbonne, 2019).

2.1.2. Vertical agreements

Article 7 of ECL, as well as Article 12 of ECLER, lay out the prohibition of anti-competitive vertical restraints.

> Article 7 of ECL:
>
> "Agreements or contracts between a Person and any of its suppliers or clients are prohibited if they are intended to restrict competition."
>
> Article 12 of ECLER:
>
> "[...]
>
> The assessment of whether the agreement or contract between a person and any of its suppliers or customers would restrict competition is based on the examination conducted by the Authority on a case-by-case basis, in light of the following factors:
>
> 1. The impact of the agreement or contract on the freedom of competition in the market.
>
> 2. The existence of benefits accrued to the consumer from the agreement or contract.
>
> 3. Considerations for maintaining product quality or reputation, security and safety requirements, in a manner that does not harm competition."

Box 2 below shows cases where ECA found violations of Article 7 of ECL.

Box 2
Selected Cases Regarding Article 7 of ECL

In 2009, ECA received a complaint that a hotel in the city of Alexandria and a photography studio had entered into an agreement granting the latter exclusive rights to provide services for weddings to the former, hence excluding all other photographers. ECA investigated the complaint and analysed the effect of the agreement on other studios, eventually issuing a violation decision against both the hotel and the studio.[66]

In 2022, ECA received a complaint regarding a school in the governorate of Fayoum, which had concluded an exclusivity agreement with a producer of school uniforms. ECA found that both the school and the producer infringed Article 7 of ECL.[67]

Most recently, in early 2024, ECA found an undertaking in the dairy sector to have concluded contracts (between 2020 and 2022) with four distributors stipulating non-compete clauses, a prohibition of passive sales, and resale price maintenance (RPM). ECA found these practices to restrict competition between the distributors and concluded that jointly with the producer they were in violation of Article 7 of ECL.

[66] ECA, Annual Report 2009, pp. 11-12. Available (in Arabic) here.
[67] ECA, ECA Continues Investigating the School Uniform Sector and Finds an Infringement of a Private School, 20 January 2022. Available (in Arabic) here.

As evident from the wording of Article 12 of ECLER, the prohibition under Article 7 of ECL requires that ECA demonstrates, at least *in abstracto*, that the agreement has actually or potentially the effect of harming competition, without however bringing into the analysis at this stage evidence of actual harm or the consideration of any economic efficiencies or justifications. It is also evident that the wording of the article is rather vague as it does not specify which types of vertical restraints may be prohibited.

A violation of Article 7 of ECL has only been found in four vertical restraints cases: there has been one case in 2009, one in 2018, and one in 2022, and one in 2024. All other vertical restraints cases were assessed under Article 8 of ECL, the undertaking in question holding a dominant position. One explanation for this is that vertical restraints were not a priority of ECA in its earlier years, given that new authorities tend to focus their enforcement on hardcore offences or those which impact inter-brand competition.[68] However, in order to minimize the resources required for ECA to prove Article 7 violations, the article should be amended so as to place a rebuttable presumption for some categories of conduct that may be harmful to competition.

For instance, the European Union generally regards RPM as a restriction of competition by-object which may in some cases (if it is a hardcore restriction) not benefit from the safe harbour of the vertical block exemption regulation.[69] The restriction of passive sales, including online sales, is also deemed to be a hardcore restriction in the European Union vertical block exemption regulation.[70] Wide "most favoured nation" (MFN) clauses may also be considered as anti-competitive by-object.[71]

ECL should therefore be amended to clearly state the categories of vertical restrictions that are more likely to be harmful to competition, creating for some of them a rebuttable presumption of being capable of producing anticompetitive effects. Accordingly, any arguments for pro-competitive effects of these agreements will need to be put forward and sufficiently substantiated by the parties to the agreement. This would facilitate ECA's work in pursuing such categories of agreements under Article 7 of ECL and will provide increased legal certainty for undertakings. The conduct listed would not be deemed *as per se* illegal, given the economic evidence that vertical restraints may under certain circumstances have pro-competitive justifications.[72] In addition, recent developments in other jurisdictions, such as recent European Union case law suggests that a vertical agreement fixing minimum resale prices (i.e. RPM) entails a "restriction of competition by object" only after having determined that that agreement presents a sufficient degree of harm to competition, taking into account the nature of its terms, the objectives that it seeks to attain and all of the factors that characterise the economic and legal context of which it forms part. As discussed further in Section 4.1, Article 7 of ECL can also include an open-ended clause covering all types of anti-competitive cooperation agreements, both horizontal and vertical, not listed under Article 6 of ECL, which will be assessed under an (actual or potential) anti-competitive effects standard.

[68] For instance, a 2020 survey shows that out of a total of 37, more jurisdictions place vertical restraints as a "low" (11) or "average" (21) priority, rather than "high" (5). See DLA Piper, Global Enforcement Priorities in Vertical Agreements, 2020. Available at: https://www.dlapiper.com/en-us/insights/publications/2024/01/global-enforcement-priorities-in-vertical-agreements.

[69] Commission Regulation (EU) 2022/720 of 10 May 2022 on the application of Article 101(3) of the Treaty on the Functioning of the European Union to categories of vertical agreements and concerted practices, Article 4(a).

[70] Commission Regulation (EU) 2022/720 of 10 May 2022 on the application of Article 101(3) of the Treaty on the Functioning of the European Union to categories of vertical agreements and concerted practices, Article 4(a). when taken into account by Egyptian competition law may still be relevant in the Egyptian market, to the extent that restricting high imports, namely by sole agents or distributors, may restrict competition from parallel imports.

[71] Note that in Germany narrow MFN clauses have also been subject to competition law prohibitions: see Federal Court of Justice, Case No. 54/20, 2021.

[72] I. Lianos, V. Korah, P. Siciliani, Competition Law: Analysis, Cases and Materials, Oxford University Press, 2019, Chapter 7.

2.1.3. Abuse of dominant position

As mentioned above, Article 8 of ECL contains a prohibition of an abuse of dominant position. This text is supplemented by Article 13 of ECLER.

Additionally, Article 4 of ECL and Articles 7 and 8 of ECLER set out the criteria for the evaluation of a dominant position in the relevant market. The first step in this test is to assess whether the undertaking has a market share of over 25 per cent. Upon establishing this limb of the test, the ECA then checks the undertaking's ability to control prices and quantities in a way that cannot be undermined by competitors. Accordingly, there is a negative presumption; establishing the market share criterion alone is not sufficient to prove that an undertaking enjoys a dominant position on the market. Likewise, a market player with a market share lower than 25 per cent, but which has the ability to unilaterally control prices and quantities, perhaps due to the nature of the product in question or the nature of the market, cannot be considered as dominant.[73] This also means that there is no possibility of rebuttal of this presumption; there is no cut off point above which, the undertaking may be considered prima facie dominant without the need to satisfy additional conditions.

The lack of a rebuttable presumption establishing dominance can risk unnecessary spending of resources. In other words, in markets where an undertaking has a very high market share, ECA must still dedicate resources to carrying out the assessment laid out in Article 13 of ECLER. As will be shown in Section 3.2.6, using resources efficiently ought to be one of ECA's priorities, given its relative lack of sufficient human and financial resources. Accordingly, multiple jurisdictions have established market share thresholds above which, undertakings are considered dominant, as shown in Section 2.3. In this context, ECL may benefit from an amendment setting this rebuttable threshold, whereas if an undertaking has a market share of less than 40 or 50 per cent, ECA would have to prove the undertaking's ability to unilaterally (or jointly with another undertaking) control price and quantity. However, in cases where the undertaking's market share goes above this threshold, the undertaking would most likely be considered dominant (a rebuttable presumption).

Note also that ECL lacks the concept of collective/joint dominance of two or more undertakings. An amendment to ECL to add the concept and criteria for collective dominance should be considered, in the situation of an oligopoly in which there may be a high likelihood of coordinated

> The exhaustive nature of market definition and market power in ECL makes them difficult to apply in markets where digital ecosystems may be present

[73] Articles 7 and 8 ECLER set out the criteria for assessment of market power:
Article 7
Dominance:
The dominance of a person in a relevant market is established with the presence of the following elements:
1. The person has a market share exceeding 25 per cent of the relevant market. The calculation of this share is based on both the relevant products and the geographical area of this market over a specific period.
2. The person's ability to exert substantial influence on the prices or the quantity supplied of the relevant products in the relevant market.
3. The inability of the competitors to limit the person's effective impact on the prices or the quantity supplied of the products in the relevant market.

Article 8:
The person is deemed to have a substantial influence on the prices or quantity supplied of the relevant products in the relevant market if this person has the ability, through their individual acts, to determine the prices or quantity supplied of these products in that market, where their competitors do not have the ability to prevent these acts, taking into consideration the following factors:
a) The person's share in the relevant market and their position in comparison to the remaining competitors.
b) The person's behaviour in the relevant market in the previous leading up to gaining the ability to set prices or control the quantity supplied.
c) The number of competing persons in the relevant market and their relative impact on the market structure.
d) The ability of the person and their competitors to access raw materials and distribution channels necessary for production.
e) The extent to which legal or actual restrictions affect the ability of a person's existing competitor to expand in the market in question or the ability of another person to enter that market.

or non-coordinated effects, even if each of the undertakings involved has on its own less than 25 per cent market share.

As for the violations listed in the body of Article 8 of ECL, it can be concluded that they cover, in an exhaustive manner, some of the most common forms of abuse of dominant position. However, the list only includes some exclusionary abuses, and excludes exploitative abuses, such as excessive pricing or unfair trading practices. This also means that certain categories of abuses associated with digital markets may also be overlooked by the provision, such as excessive data extraction, refusal to provide interoperability, or self-preferencing. Indeed, some jurisdictions have amended their competition laws to explicitly prohibit this type of behaviour. For instance, the German competition law (GWB) was amended in 2021 to give the Bundeskartellamt new powers regarding "multi-sided platforms or networks" that are "of paramount significance for competition across markets". These powers, listed in Article 19a of GWB, include prohibiting them from self-preferencing and from tying or bundling products, from refusing interoperability, and from excessive data-gathering. The amendment of Greek competition law (Law 3959/2011) proposed in 2021, included Article 2a, which prohibited "[a]ny abuse by an undertaking of its position of power in an ecosystem of structural importance to competition in the Greek territory". An "ecosystem" was described as a group of connected firms, offering different products, drawing on digital platforms to leverage their power.[74] However, the final text of the law amending Greek competition law did not include this provision. The Italian competition law was amended in 2022 to reinforce existing rules on abuse of economic dependence (which apply when there is a significant imbalance of rights and obligations without the need to demonstrate market dominance) with the establishment of a rebuttable presumption of economic dependence for customers of digital platforms when the relevant platform represents a key gateway (e.g. because of network effects) in reaching end-consumers and/or suppliers. In addition, a number of conducts were added which might be considered abuses of economic dependency particularly for digital platforms, such as (1) providing insufficient information or data on the scope or quality of the service provided, (2) imposing unjustifiably onerous contractual conditions, or (3) conducts prohibiting or making more difficult the use of alternative suppliers. Evidently, the growth of digital markets has prompted legislatures and competition authorities to envisage changes in the legislation and their practice in order to be better suited for new challenges.

This experience is also relevant in relation to Articles 3 and 4 of ECL and Articles 6 to 8 of ECLER, on defining the market and assessing market power. While these provisions have been used in the past for cases in the digital economy,[75] their exhaustive nature makes them difficult to apply in markets where digital ecosystems may be present.[76]

Therefore, while arguably, the provisions on market power as well as some clauses in Article 8 of ECL, such as Article 8(a),[77] can be stretched in scope to cover exploitative abuses, including those in digital markets, they still would not cover the practice of excessive pricing. For that reason, this practice should be included specifically in the law (see Section 2.3 for examples of

[74] Michael G. Jacobides and Ioannis Lianos, Ecosystems and Competition Law in Theory and Practice, Industrial and Corporate Change, Volume 30, Issue 5, October 2021, p. 1199-1229. Available at: https://doi.org/10.1093/icc/dtab061.

[75] There have recently been two cases relating to digital markets in which the market was defined, Uber/Careem (Box 4) and in a 2022 case regarding abuse of dominance by a food-delivery platform (see ECA, ECA Proves Violation of an Undertaking in the Food-Delivery Sector, 26 May 2022. Available (in Arabic) here.

[76] See, for instance, the recent European Commission, Market Definition Notice, (C/2024/1645) which includes a chapter on (digital) ecosystems.

[77] In a 2020 case against beverage-producer Al-Ahram, ECA found the practice of imposing retroactive rebates and margin squeeze to infringe Article 8 of ECL, although these are not explicitly listed in the law, given that they resulted in the limitation of production and distribution, in violation of Article 8(a) of ECL, and in refusal to supply, in violation of Article 8(b) of ECL. See ECA, Annual Report 2020. Available at: https://one.oecd.org/document/DAF/COMP/AR(2021)44/en/pdf. Moreover, as seen in Box 3, Article 8(a) of ECL was successfully used to cover MFNs, RPM, and restriction of passive sales.

jurisdictions who prohibit this conduct) and the scope of Article 4 of ECL should be expanded to other forms of exploitative conduct and exclusionary conduct particularly in the digital economy.

In conclusion, the presumptions relating to establishing dominance may need to be reviewed, as should perhaps the list of anti-competitive conduct included in Article 8 of ECL.

2.1.4. Merger control

As laid out above, ECA's *ex-ante* merger control system is relatively new, ECL having been amended in December 2022 (see Annex II for a more detailed explanation of the amendments). ECL takes a broad definition of "economic concentration" and covers both the acquisition of "decisive influence" (the concept of control) as well as the acquisition of material influence.[78] The concept of material influence may be inspired by the United Kingdom law and some older cases of ECL, in which ECA assessed the structural links between undertakings.[79] ECL provides for a strict standstill obligation on merging parties in case their transaction falls under the legal definition of economic concentration. ECL also introduces the possibility for ECA to impose structural and behavioural remedies. ECLER has not been amended at the time of the writing of this Report, meaning that the new additions to ECL have not yet been implemented. Ideally, ECLER would have to be amended in such a way so as to cover any areas left open to interpretation in ECL with a sufficient degree of clarity, as to reduce chances of non-compliance by undertakings, while still leaving ECA the ability to act with a level of flexibility in applying the new provisions.

It is worth noting that ECA had, previous to the amendments of the law, gathered experience in the area of merger control, namely through the following:

(1) Involvement in the healthcare sector: since August 2021, ECA has cooperated with the Ministry of Health and the Egyptian Drug Authority, as well as the General Authority for Investments, to review transactions in the healthcare sector. The health authorities, which review transactions in the sector ex-ante have been consulting with ECA on all transactions since, and ECA has issued a total of 778 decisions.[80]

(2) Cooperation with the COMESA Competition Commission: Egypt is a member State of the COMESA. As such the COMESA Competition Commission can be notified of certain transactions taking place in Egypt. In this case, the COMESA Competition Commission refers the notification file to ECA in order to conduct its assessment.[81] Since 2015, ECA has reviewed a total of 151 cases.[82] In order to comply with the COMESA Competition Regulations, ECA must remain the only point of contact for notifications referred to by the COMESA Competition Commission. This will help to prevent any procedural problems (e.g. fee division or meeting investigation deadlines) or substantive problems (e.g. the quality of assessment).

Accordingly, in relation to merger control, it is recommended that ECLER is updated to provide clarity on the novel merger control regime, and that ECA remains the focal point for the COMESA Competition Commission.

[78] Article 2 (g) of ECL. See A. Nabil, The New Egyptian Merger Control Regime: A Former Enforcer's Perspective, Competition Policy International Columns (February 2023).

[79] In this case ECA took the position that the structural links between the two undertakings led to a collusive outcome prohibited under Article 6 of ECL. See A. Nabil, The New Egyptian Merger Control Regime: A Former Enforcer's Perspective, Competition Policy International Columns (February 2023).

[80] Data obtained from ECA.

[81] COMESA Competition Regulations, Part 4.

[82] Data obtained from ECA.

2.2. Sector regulators

This sub-Section discusses the powers of Central Bank of Egypt (CBE) in relation to anti-trust violations and merger control, as well as the powers of FRA relating to merger control. It also narrates an older debate regarding competition jurisdiction over the telecommunications sector. As a general principle it is recommended to limit exemptions from competition laws and to consolidate competition enforcement under a single entity while allowing for the obtention of technical expertise and information on specific sectors by enhancing cooperation between ECA and the relevant sector-specific regulators.

2.2.1. Powers of Central Bank of Egypt (anti-competitive conduct and merger control)

Banking Law No. 194 of 2020 stipulates that banks are exempt from the application of ECL and are instead subject to competition related provisions laid out in the Banking Law and enforced by CBE. Specifically, Article 221 of this law states that institutions licensed by CBE are exempt from ECL and they are prohibited from the following activities:

(1) Agreeing to set the prices or the terms of the provision of services, agreeing to allocate markets, and conducting agreements relating to bids and tenders.

(2) The restriction of providing services for the purpose of harming consumers.

(3) Providing services for prices below cost, resulting in harm to competition.

(4) Requiring consumers or service providers to refrain from dealing with competitors with no justification.

Furthermore, according to Article 222 of this law, a specialized unit receives competition-related complaints and has the power to investigate these complaints. When a violation is established, the infringers are ordered to cease the violation before a specified date, otherwise the anti-competitive agreement would be considered null and void. The Board of the Directors of CBE can choose to impose additional measures, such as imposing a fine or disqualifying one or more directors.

It is worth noting that in most of the European Union and OECD jurisdictions, competition authorities have general competition enforcement powers across all sectors of the economy, including regulated ones (and the banking/financial sector), while ex-ante regulation is dealt with by specialised authorities. Some countries (e.g. Spain, New Zealand, Netherlands) have established integrated institutions performing the function of a sector regulator and of a competition authority, and these institutions enforce the competition law but are also being entrusted with *ex-ante* sectoral regulatory powers. Only in the United Kingdom, among OECD countries, there is concurrent jurisdiction where the Competition and Markets Authority (CMA) and the sector regulators have concurrent competition law enforcement powers. However, CMA has full jurisdiction to implement competition law rules in the banking sector and the Bank of England (the central bank in the United Kingdom) has a secondary competition objective to facilitate effective competition in the markets for services provided by persons that the Prudential Regulation Authority (PRA) authorised to carry out regulated activities.[83] Finally, there are only a few OECD countries (and only for the telecommunications sector) in which the sector regulator has competition enforcement powers in the sector (Greece, Spain).

[83] The Financial Services and Markets Act 2000 (FSMA) states that: "When discharging its general functions in a way that advances its objectives [...] the PRA must, so far as reasonably possible, act in a way that advances the following secondary objectives -
(a) the competition objective, and
(b) the competitiveness and growth objective".

wOn balance, there are significant advantages in providing sole (or concurrent) jurisdiction to competition authorities such as ECA in all sectors of the economy:[84]

Table 1
Advantages of Competition Authorities or Sector Regulators with Jurisdiction over Competition Law Matters[85]

Advantages having a system in which the sector-specific regulator has exclusive jurisdiction to implement competition rules in the specific sector	Advantages having a system in which the competition authority has sole or concurrent jurisdiction in all sectors of the economy
Sector regulators will have expert knowledge regarding the sector in question. Facilitating the consideration of competition principles by regulators when issuing technical regulations and standards.	Competition authorities have experience in enforcing competition law in different sectors. Such a system provides the advantage of the valuable expertise and experience gained by competition authorities' staff across industries. Developing such expertise within distinct sector-specific bodies may involve duplication of resources and bring about unnecessary delays. Lower risks of jurisdictional uncertainty, given that allocating competition enforcement powers between different authorities (such as in the context of converging digital markets in particular with the importance of fintech and big tech in the provision of banking and financial services[86]) may give rise to risks of overlapping jurisdiction affecting legal certainty and innovation incentives in this sector. Lower risks of inconsistent application of competition policy across sector.
	The sector regulator may be under heavy influence by the undertakings in the sector, due to ongoing cooperation. Authorities active across different industries are generally less likely to be susceptible to regulatory capture, while in the long run, sector-specific agencies may end up sharing the industry's perspective. Avoiding the risk of a less rigorous enforcement as a result of conflicting objectives and regulations: Regulatory agencies usually have wider policy concerns, such as distributional issues or a desire to correct market failures besides the existence of market power and such concerns might lead them to tolerate or encourage anti-competitive market structures when they are deemed necessary to achieve broader policy objectives; something that may reduce competition.
Facilitating the application of a changing optimal blend of competition law enforcement and regulatory solutions. Sector regulators may therefore choose the most appropriate regime, under the regulatory statute or competition law, to tackle a particular problem.	The priorities of competition enforcement are more easily aligned if enforcement in all sectors is through a single competition regulator.
	In cases of concurrent jurisdiction, the competition authority and the sector regulator may not always be inclined to cooperate.

84 Independent Sector Regulators - Note by BIAC, OECD Working Party No. 2 on Competition and Regulation, 2019. Available at: https://one.oecd.org/document/DAF/COMP/WP2/WD(2019)34/en/pdf.

85 The table is inspired by the Independent Sector Regulators - Note by BIAC, OECD Working Party No. 2 on Competition and Regulation, 2019. Available at: https://one.oecd.org/document/DAF/COMP/WP2/WD(2019)34/en/pdf; and Letter of Frederic Jenny to the Chairman of the Hellenic Competition Commission, COMP/2020.114.

86 See A. Nabil, The New Egyptian Merger Control Regime: A Former Enforcer's Perspective, Competition Policy International Columns (February 2023), noting "[t]his is another controversial point of law to the extent that it does not clearly define which activities fall under the authority of ECA and which fall under the supervision of FRA. For instance, it is not uncommon that economic operators who are active in the services sector may offer, for example, fintech services (an FRA activity) among other services (non-FRA activities), yet the majority of its turnover is generated from non-FRA activities. How such a case will be treated, remains unsettled".

Reflecting on the above, it is apparent that although the jurisdiction of CBE on competition rules may have limited advantages, as CBE naturally has experience in the banking sector, but that granting exclusive jurisdiction to the competition authority may be more beneficial for consumers and in integrating competition principles in the banking sector. For that reason, exclusive jurisdiction over competition matters should be granted to ECA.

Alternatively, there should be cooperation between CBE and ECA in order to ensure consistency and legal certainty in the application of competition laws, should the special regime for CBE be maintained. The conclusion of formal MoUs between the two institutions so that ECA may express its views in competition proceedings undertaken in the banking sector to CBE may provide a step towards more intensive cooperation.

2.2.2. Powers of Financial Regulatory Authority (merger control)

Articles 19 bis e and 19 bis f of ECL address the procedures of economic concentrations in the financial non-banking sector. Economic concentrations where the target firm operates in the financial non-banking sector are notified to FRA before the conclusion of the contract. FRA is mandated to request ECA's opinion, although the opinion is not binding. ECA must issue its opinion within 30 calendar days of receiving the notification of the transaction from FRA. All other competition matters in the financial non-banking sector, however, are handled by ECA. As such, in order to promote consistency across competition-related decisions in the sector, and across all sectors, this parallel merger control regime - which has not yet been implemented in practice, as ECLER has not yet been updated, should be abolished.

Alternatively, the system would require clear guidelines for the cooperation between FRA and ECA, or the conclusion of an MoU between ECA and FRA, as well as involvement of ECA experts in the decision-making process of FRA.

2.2.3. The telecommunications sector

The National Telecom Regulatory Authority (NTRA) was established in 2003 through Law No. 10 of 2003. The law states that NTRA's mission is to "regulate the telecom sector [...] and to encourage national and international investments in the sector considering free competition rules [...]", but it does not give it any substantive or enforcement powers relating to competition. Nevertheless, the two authorities seemed to disagree upon who had the jurisdiction over competition matters in the telecommunications sector. The matter, however, was settled with a 2013 decision by the Economic Court of Appeal. In that case, ECA had referred two mobile operators to the courts for non-compliance with ECA in the context of a cartel investigation. When the Court of First Instance ruled for a fine under Article 22 bis of ECL, the undertakings argued that ECA did not have the jurisdiction to refer them to the court in the first place. The Economic Court of Appeal upheld the Court of First Instance's decision, reiterating that ECA enjoyed sole jurisdiction over this sector for competition law enforcement regardless of the fact that NTRA implemented telecommunication regulation in it.[87]

ECA has since carried out work in the sector as for any other sector of the economy, and in 2021, the two authorities signed an addendum to an older MoU they had concluded, with the aim of increasing coordination and cooperation. Further, a joint committee was established

[87] Eslam Mostafa Saleh, Intra-governmental Struggle for Power Between Competition Authority and Telecommunication Regulator: A Story From Egypt, Kluwer Competition Law Blog, 23 November 2021. Available at: https://competitionlawblog.kluwercompetitionlaw.com/2021/11/23/intra-governmental-struggle-for-power-between-competition-authority-and-telecommunication-regulator-a-story-from-egypt/#_ftnref13.

between the two entities, tasked with discussing issues of common interest.[88] In June 2023, ECA issued joint guidelines with NTRA addressed to market players in the telecommunications market, providing guidance on avoiding ECL infringements in the context of providing services to closed urban complexes. The guidelines generally aim to promote having more than one service provider to operate in a complex, reducing the expenses of service providers in terms of supporting infrastructure sharing, and promoting investment in core network equipment, for the benefit of stakeholders in the telecommunications services market, potential competitors, and consumers. ECA also held a roundtable with different stakeholders in order to explain the guidelines.

2.3. Reflections: comparison to international best practices

Following the assessment above, Table 2 summarises some observations and recommendations regarding ECL, and compares them to international best practices.

Table 2
Substantive Aspects of ECL Compared to Other Jurisdictions

Status quo/suggestion	Examples from other jurisdictions
Article 6 of ECL	
Article 6 of ECL offers an exhaustive list of anti-competitive conduct between competitors and does not differentiate between types of horizontal agreements. The conduct can instead be split into hardcore and non-hardcore violations, either in ECL or in soft law.	(1) The European Union: the European Commission's Guidelines on the applicability of Article 101 of TFEU to horizontal co-operation agreements, the last version of which was published in 2023, set out a list of hardcore restrictions, as well as the criteria used to determine whether an agreement is a by-object restriction. Article 101 of TFEU itself does not provide an exhaustive list of prohibited practices. (2) The United Kingdom: The United Kingdom CMA sets out in its Guidance on Horizontal Agreements (2023) a differentiation between by-object and by-effect violations, elaborating on the prohibitions set out in Section 2 of the Competition Act 1998. Again, there is no exhaustive list of prohibited practices. (3) India: Chapter II of the Indian Competition Act 2002 generally prohibits agreements between competitors regarding "production, supply, distribution, storage, acquisition or control of goods or provision of services", if it is likely to cause an appreciable adverse effect on competition within India. It then goes on to state that certain horizontal agreements are "presumed to have an appreciable adverse effect on competition", namely those regarding price-setting, limiting production, market allocation, and bid-rigging. (4) Singapore: the Competition and Consumer Commission of Singapore sets out in its Guidelines on the Section 34, a list of 11 practices that are prohibited between competitors, and states that the first four types - "sharing markets, limiting or controlling production or investment, fixing trading conditions, and joint purchasing or selling" - are considered restrictive to competition "by their very nature".

[88] Interactions Between Competition Authorities and Sector Regulators - Contribution from Egypt, 2022, p. 3. Available at: https://one.oecd.org/document/DAF/COMP/GF/WD(2022)10/en/pdf.

Article 6 of ECL only mentions contracts and agreements and does not refer to decisions by associations of undertakings or concerted practices.	(1) The European Union: Article 101 of TFEU clearly sets out that prohibited conduct includes "all agreements between undertakings, decisions by associations of undertakings and concerted practices [...]". The European Union courts have interpreted these concepts in a rather liberal way, and also allow for the simultaneous qualification of conduct as being an "agreement and/or concerted practice". [89] (2) South Africa: Section 4 of the Competition Act (No. 89 of 1998) prohibits "An agreement between, or concerted practice by, firms, or a decision by an association of firms [...]". To entrench this further, of Section 4(2) sets out that an agreement between two or more firms is presumed if "(a) anyone of those firms owns a significant interest in the other, or they have at least one director or substantial shareholder in common; and (b) any combination of those firms engages in that restrictive horizontal practice".
Article 7 of ECL	
Article 7 of ECL currently does not lay out the types of vertical restraints that are considered harmful to competition. These should be listed either in the law or in soft laws. Further, the most harmful types of vertical restraints should be considered by-object violations, namely: RPM[90], wide MFN clauses, and restrictions of passive sales leading to absolute territorial protection.	(1) Australia: The Australian Competition and Consumer Act (2003) explicitly prohibits RPM in Section 48: "A corporation or other person shall not engage in the practice of resale price maintenance". (2) Canada: The Canadian law outlaws any type of "price maintenance", and not just RPM, by stating in Section 76(1) of the Competition Act (1985) that a person violates the law if they "(i) by agreement, threat, promise or any like means, has influenced upward, or has discouraged the reduction of, the price at which the person's customer or any other person to whom the product comes for resale supplies or offers to supply or advertises a product within Canada, or (ii) has refused to supply a product to or has otherwise discriminated against any person or class of persons engaged in business in Canada because of the low pricing policy of that other person or class of persons". (3) China: Following a landmark decision of the Supreme People's Court in China in Hainan Provincial Price Bureau v. Hainan Yutai Scientific Feed Company, the Amended Anti-Monopoly Law of China (Article 18) of 2022 introduced a provision which states that a monopoly agreement between counterparties fixing the price or setting a minimum price for resale of goods to a third party "shall not be prohibited if the undertaking can prove that it does not have the effect of eliminating or restricting competition." Hence, although Chinese competition authority may rely on the presumption that RPM agreements eliminate or restrict competition and conclude that they are illegal, this is a rebuttable presumption if the defendant undertaking adduces sufficient evidence to prove that the RPM agreement does not eliminate or restrict competition. (4) The Netherlands: While the Netherlands abides by the regulations and guidance issued by the European Commission, it has published its own guidelines on vertical restraints, explicitly designating RPM, market-sharing, restriction of passive sales, and restriction of online sales as hard-core restrictions.[91]

89 See Case T-186/06, Solvay SA v Commission (2011) ECR II-2839, paragraphs 91-2 ("[i] n the context of a complex infringement which involved many producers seeking over a number of years to regulate the market between them, the Commission cannot be expected to classify the infringement precisely, as an agreement or concerted practice, as in any event both those forms of infringement are covered by Article [101(1) of TFEU] [...]"). See also Case T-235/07, Bavaria v Commission (2011) ECR II-3229, paragraph 183. The twofold characterisation of the infringement as an agreement "and/or" concerted practice must be understood as referring to a complex whole comprising a number of factual elements some of which were characterised as agreements and others as concerted practices for the purposes of Article [101(1) of TFEU], which lays down no specific category for a complex infringement of this type. Subsequent jurisprudence of the European Union Courts has made it clear that decisions of association of undertakings may also be included in the characterization: see Case T-410/09, Almanet v Commission, ECLI:EU:T:2012:676, paragraph 152, the court noting that according to settled case law, the concept of a single infringement can be applied to the legal characterisation of anti- competitive conduct consisting in agreements, in concerted practices and in decisions of associations of undertakings.

90 Although this does not mean that RPM are considered automatically as "hardcore restrictions of competition": see Case C-211/22, Super Bock, ECLI:EU:C:2023:529. According to the CJEU (paragraph 41), "the concepts of 'hardcore restrictions' and of 'restriction by-object' are not conceptually interchangeable and do not necessarily overlap. It is therefore necessary to examine restrictions falling outside that exemption, on a case-by-case basis, with regard to Article 101 (1) TFEU".

91 Authority for Consumers and Markets, Arrangements between suppliers and buyers, 2019, pp. 5-7. Available at: https://www.acm.nl/sites/default/files/documents/2019-07/guidelines-regarding-arrangements-between-suppliers-and-buyers.pdf.

Article 8 of ECL	
There is currently an irrebuttable presumption that undertakings with a market share below 25 per cent, but with the ability to control price and quantity, are not considered dominant. This should be replaced by a rebuttable market share threshold over which the undertaking is presumed to be dominant.	(1) Germany: GWB (1958, as amended in October 2023) Section 18(4) provides: "An undertaking is considered to be dominant if it has a market share of at least 40 percent" or if it, according to paragraph (1) "has no competitors, is not exposed to any substantial competition, or has a paramount market position in relation to its competitors". (2) Russian Federation: Federal Law No. 135-FZ (2006) designates in Article 5 that undertakings, other than financial organizations, will be considered dominant if their market share is above 50 per cent, and may be considered dominant if their market share is below that threshold, depending on the market shares of its competitors and the barriers to entry. (3) Saudi Arabia: the Implementing Regulations of the Saudi Competition Law (2019) state in Article 10 that dominance is achieved by having a market share above 40 per cent and/or having the ability to control prices, production, or demand.
Exploitative abuses, such as excessive pricing, should be added to the list of practices prohibited for dominant undertakings.	(1) South Africa: Sec 8(1)(a) of the Competition Act (No. 89 of 1998) prohibits dominant firms from charging "an excessive price to the detriment of consumers or customers". (2) The European Union and the United Kingdom: while these jurisdictions do not explicitly prohibit excessive pricing in legislation, case law and precedent shows that it can be considered as an instance of abuse of dominant position.[92]

In conclusion, this part of the Report has analysed the different substantive aspects of ECL, offering some comparisons to the practices of other jurisdictions. The following Section turns to the analysis the procedures laid out in ECL, and accordingly the powers and procedures of ECA and other relevant governmental institutions.

92 CJEU, Case 27/76 United Brands Company and United Brands Co BV vs. Commission of the European Communities (1978); and CMA, Case 505905 Excessive and unfair pricing with respect to the supply of liothyronine tablets in the United Kingdom, 2021.

Chapter III

Institutional design

The ECA is the sole governmental institution responsible for applying ECL. However, in its application, challenges arise in enforcement structures and practices, including fines calculation, imposition of administrative monetary sanctions and binding remedies, limiting its effectiveness. Regarding the institution itself, ECA's lack of independence, budget and staffing issues could impact its operational capacity. ECA's private enforcement of competition laws is also underdeveloped, which limit the effectiveness of compensating victims of anti-competitive practices.

3. Institutional design

As explained throughout this Report, ECA is the sole governmental institution responsible for applying ECL. ECL lays the framework for ECA's structure, power, and relationship with other governmental and judicial institutions. The following sub-Section looks into the role of different state institutions in the enforcement of ECL, mainly by also exploring the fining powers of the courts, followed by a sub-Section on ECA.

3.1. Enforcement structures and practices

Article 21 of ECL, in its current version, lays out that only ECA can initiate criminal proceedings against an infringing undertaking. Accordingly, the public prosecution then takes over the case, utilizing the facts gathered and the analysis carried out by ECA, as well as carrying out further investigation if necessary. If the public prosecution finds merit in the case, it raises it to the economic court, which assesses the case at first instance. In turn, if the court upholds ECA's decision, it can fine the undertaking, in line with the fines laid out in ECL. Accordingly, three aspects of this system are worth exploring further: (1) the fines and settlement amounts laid out in ECL, (2) the fact that ECA itself does not have fining powers, including the power to issue administrative fines, and (3) the question of employing non-pecuniary penalties.

3.1.1. Determining settlement amounts and fines

The fines for the substantive ECL infringements, issued by the court, and the settlement amounts, issued by ECA, are currently laid out in Articles 21 and 22 of ECL. They can be an absolute value or a percentage of the revenue of the product subject to the violation (rather than all the products in the relevant market) during the period at stake, both within specified ranges. The latter option namely, although perhaps more reflective of the revenue earned from the anti-competitive practice, presents multiple practical difficulties.

For instance, it can be difficult in some cases to ascertain the duration of the infringement. An example of this is an anti-competitive agreement in violation to Article 6 of ECL. As explained above, the agreement does not have to be implemented in order to be considered a violation under ECL. In this case, it would be difficult to determine the duration of the agreement, as it technically did not last beyond the initial concurrence of wills. A similar problem occurs with determining the product subject to the violation, as it may not, according to the current wording of the article, include all the products included in the relevant market. An example of this is a case of predatory pricing of an electronic appliance, for instance, where, for any reason, not all units of this electronic appliance were sold at the predatory price during the period of the infringement. In that case, while the market is defined to be that of the appliance, the total revenue of the sales of the appliance will not be taken into account when determining the fine, but rather only the units sold at the low price. It may be difficult to ascertain, or at least mathematically distinguish, the specific products that were subject to the violation.

Similarly, in some cases, it may be difficult to practically calculate the revenues of a certain product, especially if it is sold in a bundle. In other cases, such as those of predatory pricing, determining the product may be easy, but calculating the fine based on a percentage of its sales may be disproportionate to the harm caused to the market, as the price of the product is subject to predatory pricing will have been artificially low. The same concern pertains to a bid-rigging agreement in which one of the infringing undertakings agrees not to enter the bid.

A natural solution in these cases would be to resort to the absolute value option. Indeed, the court has in fact used that method of setting fines in most of its decisions regarding ECL. This reinstates the point that the practical issues associated with the calculation of a fine as a portion of revenues can result in institutions resorting to fines that may not necessarily reflect the anti-competitive harm, but also not be sufficiently deterrent, which is arguably not what was intended by the legislature.

ECA, on the contrary, usually resorts to the percentage option when calculating settlement amounts. This could be due to a preference to be more cautious with the application of ECL; given that Article 22 of ECL states that this option should only be used if it is "not possible to calculate" the revenues, and it is perhaps safer to abide by the percentage option unless absolutely necessary. In the examples provided in the previous paragraphs, it would be difficult to argue that the revenue cannot be calculated, meaning that ECA could, potentially, issue a settlement amount of EGP 0 for an anti-competitive agreement that was never implemented.

A solution for this would be to amend ECL to state that in cases where the fine or settlement amount, under the percentage option, would amount to EGP 0, the absolute value should be used. Another solution may be simplifying the percentage option so that it is easier for courts to apply and less problematic for ECA. By surveying international best practices, the United Kingdom CMA's fining methodology serves as an example that avoids most of the problems identified above. The 2021 fining Guidelines lay out that CMA will (usually) start with a base of 30 per cent of the undertaking's relevant turnover.[93] More specifically, the relevant turnover is the turnover of the undertaking in the relevant product and geographic market, in the business year preceding the infringement.[94] This bypasses the issue of having to specify the exact products that were subject to the infringement, as well as having to ascertain the duration of the anti-competitive practice. To avoid the issue which relates to predatory pricing, CMA allows for an adjustment for the penalty on a case-by-case basis, namely for "any gain which might accrue to the undertaking in other product or geographic markets as well as the "relevant" market under consideration".[95] Overall, however, there is a maximum cap of 10 per cent of the undertaking's worldwide turnover in the last business year.[96]

Similarly, the competition law in Saudi Arabia ensures simplicity regarding the duration of the infringement in a similar manner; by calculating the revenue based on the infringement.[97] Competition law in India utilizes an arguably simpler methodology of placing a maximum of 10 per cent of the "average of the turnover for the last three preceding financial years".[98]

The United States offers the example of a jurisdiction which adopts a prosecutorial model, as does Egypt, although in the United States, cartels are prosecuted as criminal offenses, and sentences are imposed by a non-specialized court. According to the United States Sentencing Guidelines (USSG), both pecuniary and non-pecuniary penalties may be imposed: fines on firms and individuals, as well as imprisonment of individuals involved in the cartel. To determine the base fine, a percentage of the *volume of affected commerce*, that is, of total sales from the relevant market (t), is taken into account. The USSG suggests that 20 per cent of the volume of affected commerce can be used as a good proxy ($f\,b=0.2t$). This volume of affected commerce covers the entire duration of the infringement. Once the amount of the base fine has been calculated, aggravating and mitigating elements are taken into consideration. However, the

93 CMA, CMA's guidance as to the appropriate amount of a penalty, 2021, paragraphs 2.01-2.09. Available at: https://assets.publishing.service.gov.uk/media/622f73c58fa8f56c170b7274/CMA73final_.pdf.

94 Ibid, paragraph 2.10.

95 Ibid, paragraphs 2.22-2.23.

96 A similar approach is also adopted in the European Union: see the European Guidelines on the Method of Setting Fines (2006).

97 Article 19 of Saudi Arabian Competition Law (2019).

98 Section 27(b) of Indian Competition Act 12 of 2003 (2002).

final fine for undertakings must not exceed a maximum statutory limit which is the greatest of 100 million US$ or twice the gross pecuniary gains the violators derived from the cartel or twice the gross pecuniary loss caused to the victims. As USSG chapter 2 indicates, "the purpose for specifying a percent of the volume of commerce is to avoid the time and expense that would be required for the court to determine the actual gain or loss".

For these reasons, an amendment to the fining methodology set out in ECL should be considered.

An additional issue relates to the wording of Article 21 of ECL, as well as the general legal regime, which (according to the dominant interpretation adopted by ECA) dictates that, in order for a settlement request to be approved, all parties to the infringement must agree to settle. For instance, in cases of Article 6 of ECL violation, *all* parties to a cartel must submit a request for settlement in order for it to be presented to the Board. This excludes hybrid settlements, that is settlements by only some of the members of the cartel.[99] The inability to proceed with hybrid settlements may result in situations where cases are referred to public prosecution because one party refuses to settle, prolonging the decision-making process for the rest of the infringers who were otherwise willing to cooperate with ECA. Hybrid settlements present several challenges and problems, such as the protection of the rights of defence of the non-settling parties, the right to good administration and the presumption of innocence[100] and issues regarding the interaction between public and private enforcement. In addition to the reduced procedural efficiency of hybrid settlement decisions, but in view of the fact that ECA will not avoid the possibility of appeals to the decision concerning the non-settling parties if there is an infringement, it is therefore important to provide ECA the discretion to make the choice of settling with some of the defendants on a case-by-case basis using hybrid settlements. In that light, ECL should be amended to allow for hybrid settlements for competition violations.

Finally, the monetary amount of these fines, especially those of absolute value, should be revised in the context of recent economic changes. As explained above, the last amendments to the fines were carried out through the 2014 law amendments, i.e. preceding the floating of the Egyptian pound, starting in 2016. Changes in the value of the currency, as well as rising global inflation, may mean that the current monetary amounts of fines are not sufficiently deterrent and should be revised.

It becomes apparent from the above that the current fining system is associated with some practical difficulties, which may be resolved by employing a simpler methodology that is based on the turnover of the products in the relevant market for a set period of years. Similarly, there should be some changes to settlement procedures as described above. The fine amounts should also be increased to enhance deterrence.

3.1.2. Administrative monetary sanctions

ECA does not currently have the power to issue administrative monetary sanctions to the extent that competition law enforcement is based on a prosecutorial criminal justice model. Granting courts the sole jurisdiction to rule on criminal cases comes with a number of benefits and drawbacks.

Naturally, courts are constitutionally independent from other non-judiciary institutions, which would guarantee impartiality when applying the provisions of ECL. Courts are also accountable; decisions can be appealed and seen by higher courts. However, courts are also naturally less

[99] In the European Union, the first hybrid settlement case was Animal Feed Phosphates: Commission Decision of 20 July 2010 in Animal Feed Phosphates (Case COMP/AT.38866). The European Commission has adopted nine hybrid settlement decisions for cartels. Note that the Commission had adopted 38 cartel settlement decisions between 2008-2021.

[100] See, for instance, Case C883/19 P, HSBC Holdings v. Commission, ECLI:EU:C:2023:11.

specialized than competition authorities in competition matters. While the Economic Courts, established in 2008,[101] specialize in commercial and financial matters such as those relating to banking, insurance, leasing, investment, consumer protection, and insolvency, but are not necessarily familiar with competition law and policy.[102] The courts have been seen to rely on expert witnesses specializing in competition economics, but decisions are ultimately made by legal experts who may have not previously dealt with competition matters. Furthermore, court decisions arguably take longer to be finalized, compared to those of an administrative authority, as they move through the process of public prosecution and court hearings. To illustrate, it is worth noting that concerning the duration of the eight cases referred to the courts, the average time from the date of the issue of ECA's decision to a final decision (i.e. that of the highest court to rule on the issue) was three years and nine months. The longest duration was eight years. This can reduce deterrence, as the infringing undertakings will likely have benefited from the rents they reaped from the conduct violating ECL before finally paying a fine. For comparison purposes, the average duration of a settlement decision by ECA is seven months and 18 days.

Table 3
Decisions on Fines and Settlements (2006-2023)

Year	Total number of court decisions and total fine amount[103]	Total number of settlement decisions
2006		1
2007		1
2008		1
2009		1
2010		1
2011		3
2012		5
2013		4
2014	1 (EGP 200,000,000/ US$ 4,263,160)	7
2015		22
2016		15
2017		12
2018		1
2019	1 (EGP 1,400,000,000/ US$ 29,844,220)	1
2020	2 (EGP 400,000,000/ US$ 8,527,825)	1
2021	2 (EGP 400,000,000/ US$ 8,527,825)	1
2022	1 (EGP 200,000,000/ US$ 4,264,022)	1
2023		3

101 Law No. 120 of 2008 Establishing the Economic Courts.

102 The need for specialized training of the judges of the Economic Court in competition law and economics matters was highlighted by the interviewee from the business association, who also noted the importance of building up expertise over time by allocating the competition law related cases to a small pool of judges of the Economic Court.

103 For cases that have been through several levels of the court, this table only accounts for the decisions of the highest level of the court, and the fine issued by that court.

It may be worth considering a mechanism by which ECA can issue administrative monetary sanctions for undertakings violating ECL, and for those who fail to implement ECA's decisions, in parallel to the criminal route, which prosecutes individuals in court. This can be seen in various competition regimes in the Middle East, such as Kuwait[104] and Saudi Arabia.[105] The United Kingdom CMA[106] and the European Commission[107] also have the power to adopt administrative monetary sanctions on their own accord. Proposals have also been made in the United States to provide the United States Federal Trade Commission and the United States Department of Justice the power to impose civil monetary penalties for violations of the Sherman Act or Federal Trade Commission Act.[108] On the national level, the Board of Directors of CBE also enjoys the power to impose administrative monetary sanctions on undertakings.[109]

Furthermore, the concerns relating to the independence and impartiality of ECA that would act as investigator/prosecutor and decision-maker do not stand serious scrutiny (as there are other jurisdictions with a similar integrated agency structure, such as the European Commission, or the United Kingdom CMA) and in any case may be resolved with amendments to enhance the Board's independence (see Section 3.2.1). However, if the impartiality of an integrated administrative agency raises concerns, these may be addressed through some institutional changes, such as adding an independent grievance committee, eventually within ECA's structure. The committee would be made up of professionals or experts in the field of competition law and economics.[110] Similar models of specialised tribunals appear in the Cartel Court in Austria, the Market Court in Sweden, or the United Kingdom Competition Appeal Tribunal. Since the decisions issued by this committee would be administrative in nature, it would be held accountable in a manner similar to that relating to ECA's Board today, as explained in Section 1.4.1.

Moreover, to ensure transparency, ECA could issue a policy document or guidelines on the methodology of determining administrative monetary sanctions, to be followed by the Board. This approach is often followed by young but also more mature competition authorities in order to promote a more objective assessment and transparency in setting fines.[111]

In summary, giving ECA's Board the power to issue administrative monetary sanctions can expedite procedures, ensure greater deterrence, while utilizing the expertise of ECA without risking impartiality in decision-making.

3.1.3. Alternative sanctions

ECL currently only allows for pecuniary individual penalties for infringements relating to anti-trust and merger control. Additionally, Article 50 of Law No. 182 of 2018 Regulating Contracts by Public Entities lays out separate sanctions relating to bid-rigging, whereas those found to partake in bid-rigging can be barred from participating in future public procurement tenders. This sub-Section further explores the idea of adding such debarment sanctions to ECL, as well as the criminal sanction of imprisonment.

[104] Articles 32 to 34 of Law No. 72/2020 for the Protection of Competition (2020).
[105] Article 18 of Saudi Arabian Competition Law (2019).
[106] Section 36 of Competition Act 1998.
[107] Council Regulation (EC) No 1/2003 of 16 December 2002 on the implementation of the rules on competition laid down in Articles 81 and 82 of the Treaty.
[108] See H. First, The Case for Antitrust Civil Penalties, 76(1) Antitrust Law Journal 127, 2009.
[109] Article 144(h) of Banking Law No. 194 of 2020.
[110] Such committees would be created in a similar manner to those created for merger control decisions, as per Article 27 of ECLER. According to the article, they would report to and be supervised by ECA's Board. These committees would not take the form of extra-judicial courts or tribunals, as those are prohibited via Article 96 of the Constitution. External members can be added to these committees according to Article 13 of ECL, which states that: "[t]he Board may invite specialists to attend its meeting of whom it wishes to seek assistance. Such specialists shall not have a counted vote".
[111] OECD, Sanctions in Antitrust Cases - Background Paper by the Secretariat, 2016. Available at: https://one.oecd.org/document/DAF/COMP/GF(2016)6/en/pdf.

Debarment sanctions, such as exclusion from public procurement and director disqualification, are utilized by some jurisdictions against undertakings and individuals, respectively, with the objective of deterrence. The former is indeed included in the Egyptian regime, while the latter is not. Director disqualification is an individual sanction applied to the managers or directors of undertakings participating in anti-competitive practices, most often cartels, prohibiting them from occupying similar positions for a set number of years. The aim of this sanction is often deterrence, as well as the protection of the public from further misconduct by individuals who previously carried out anti-competitive practices.[112] It can be used as a stand-alone sanction or in combination with other sanctions. Jurisdictions that employ this sanction include Australia, Canada, Germany, and the United Kingdom.[113] The aim of individual deterrence is integral to Egypt's competition law regime, so this sanction should be considered, but its length and application should be limited to account for the special characteristics of the Egyptian economy, including the prevalence of family businesses.[114]

Moreover, similar sanctions with the aim of "naming-and-shaming" directors can be employed, by publishing a list of those found to have infringed the law. Given that ECL sanctions individuals, as explained in Section 1.4, it is in line with the spirit of the law in identifying the directors responsible for the management of an undertaking and publish their names along with infringement decisions or a press release. It would also increase specific and general deterrence, which is often the goal of criminal enforcement models. ECA could also perhaps employ a "Legality Rating" system, as in Italy, where undertakings can be given a star rating following an assessment of competition laws by the Italian Competition Authority.[115]

Notably, imprisonment, which is referred to in the law of several jurisdictions such as the United Kingdom and the United States, may not fit in ECL. In fact, in debating the first version of ECL in 2005, the Egyptian parliament considered adding imprisonment as a sanction, but eventually decided against it, the most prominent argument being that financial sanctions would be more appropriate in the law's nascent years.[116] It was also mentioned during the debates[117] that the option nonetheless exists through Article 345 of Penal Code, which states that "[p]ersons who caused an increase or decrease in the prices of crops or goods or coupons or tradable bonds than their actual commercial value through spreading on purpose false information or news paying the retailer a price which is higher than the price he requested (to cause an inflation in prices) or through conspiring with famous trader who holds one item of any goods or crops in order to make them not to sell their products in the first place or to stop them from selling to others on a price that is lower than that they agreed upon between each other or by any other or any other deceitful method, shall be imprisoned for not more than one year and a fine not exceeding EGP 500 (US$ 11) or one of those sanctions only". Article 346 adds: "[t]he celling determined for the penalty of detection as prescribed in the previous Article shall be doubled if that fraud occurs in regard to the prices of meat, bread, fuel wood, and coal, or other like of necessities".

[112] OECD, Director Disqualification and Bidder Exclusion in Competition Enforcement - Background Note by the Secretariat, 2022, p. 10. Available at: https://one.oecd.org/document/DAF/COMP(2022)14/en/pdf.

[113] Ibid.

[114] 80 per cent of Egypt's national income and 75 per cent of its private sector economy is attributable to family businesses, and 45 per cent of family businesses do not employ a Board of Directors, meaning that the shareholders are often the directors of the company. See Statement by Executive Director of the Egyptian Centre for Arbitration and Settlement of Non-Banking Financial Disputes (ECAS), 2023. Available at: https://www.egypttoday.com/Article/3/128182/Family-businesses-represent-nearly-80-of-Egypt%E2%80%99s-national-income; and PwC, Egypt Family Business Survey, 2021. Available at: https://www.pwc.com/m1/en/publications/family-business-survey/egypt-family-business-survey/documents/egypt-family-business-survey-2021.pdf.

[115] Italy, Decree Law No. 214/2011.

[116] Official Gazette, 8th Term of Assembly of the People's Assembly of the Arab Republic of Egypt, 5th Ordinary Meeting, 27th Session (17 January 2005), 12 February 2005, p. 63-64.

[117] Ibid., p. 63.

Accordingly, given the principle that the stricter sanction prevails, it could be argued that as it currently stands, the Egyptian courts could impose a one-to-two-year prison sentence in the presence of a violation of Article 6 of ECL. It is worth noting that these articles have not been applied regarding violations of ECL since its promulgation.[118]

As such, it is recommended that ECL is amended to provide for individual, non-pecuniary sanctions.

Following the above analysis of the sanctions associated with anti-competitive conduct, the next Section will delve more into the role of ECA in enforcing competition law.

3.2. Egyptian Competition Authority

ECA formally began carrying out its mandate in 2006. ECA's powers are derived from Article 11 of ECL. Arguably, the focus on different powers has changed over time since its creation. Since 2021, the 2021-2025 Strategy has clearly laid out ECA's mission and vision as follows:

ECA's Vision:	**ECA's Mission:**
Raising the efficacy and robustness of the Egyptian economy by stirring competition in the markets.	Instilling competition policy by curbing anti-competitive practices and opening markets to new competitors with reduced barriers to entry while guaranteeing competitive neutrality, thus ensuring a competitive market that improves the welfare of consumers, businesses, and the national economy.

This Section discusses ECA's independence, investigation powers, role in market monitoring, limiting anti-competitive state measures, and on the international sphere, as well as its resources and enforcement record.

3.2.1. Institutional independence

As discussed above, ECA benefits from a certain degree of independence, evidenced through its autonomous budget and its power to unilaterally issue administrative decisions (such as interim measures or infringement decisions). Overall, independence can be seen to empower a competition authority not only in terms of reputation, but it has also been empirically proven to enhance its performance.[119] Indeed, the importance of empowering ECA seems to have been a priority since its creation: transcripts of early discussions of drafts of ECL suggest a consensus that, "This Authority is important, and if it is not given power, an independent budget being a source of power, it will become weak".[120] However, ECA still lacks independence regarding two key aspects: its formal affiliation to the Prime Minister, undermining the independence that should be granted to it under the Egyptian Constitution, and the composition of its Board of Directors.

Article 215 of the Egyptian Constitution states that, "[i]ndependent bodies and regulatory agencies are identified by law. These bodies and agencies have legal personality, and technical, financial and administrative independence, and are consulted about draft laws and regulations that relate to their fields of operation. These bodies and agencies include the Central Bank, the Egyptian

[118] Mahmoud A Momtaz, Revisiting the Imprisonment Sentence under the Egyptian Competition Regime, World Competition, Volume 40, Issue 4, 2017, p. 637-654, 644.

[119] See, for instance, Mattia Guidi, Does Independence Affect Regulatory Performance? The case of national competition authorities in the European Union, EUI Working Papers, 2011. Available at: https://www.researchgate.net/publication/254411520_Does_Independence_Affect_Regulatory_Performance_The_case_of_national_competition_authorities_in_the_European_Union.

[120] Official Gazette, 8th Term of Assembly of the People's Assembly of the Arab Republic of Egypt, 5th Ordinary Meeting, 27th Session (17 January 2005), 12 February 2005, p. 17.

Financial Supervisory Authority, the Central Auditing Organization, and the Administrative Control Authority". These are affiliated with the Head of State (the President of the Republic). The list of entities is evidently non-exhaustive, and could potentially include ECA, especially given that it fulfils the criteria listed in the article. According to Article 216 of the Constitution, however, this would explicitly need to be laid out in ECL. Notably, as mentioned in Section 1.2, the Constitution also highlights the importance of maintaining competition in its Article 27. As the Constitution contains specific provisions for the creation of independent supervisory bodies (Articles 215 and 216), and to the extent that ECA carries out similar supervisory mandates as the abovementioned supervisory bodies, it should follow the same institutional structure in order to avoid any situation of conflict of interest, in particular in cases of competitive neutrality.

However, ECA does not enjoy the same degree of independence as the abovementioned supervisory authorities in the way this is defined in the Egyptian Constitution, as it is affiliated with the "competent minister". As explained in Section 1.3, this affiliation is imposed by Article 11, which states that ECA is affiliated with the competent minister, defined in Article 2 of ECL's preamble as the Prime Minister (between 2006 and 2022 the Minister of Trade and Industry was following delegation and acting as the ministerial sponsoring government department). In contrast, other key state institutions, such as CBE and the Central Auditing Organization, follow the constitutional requirements for independence and are affiliated directly with the Head of State.[121]

While the affiliation of competition authorities differs from one jurisdiction to another - some being completely non-ministerial, such as the CMA[122] and others are required to take instruction from the government in some situations - key institutions in the Egyptian state are empowered in terms of their policy impact under Articles 215 and 216 of the Egyptian Constitution and are accordingly supported by the Head of State. Granting ECA the independence stipulated for it in the Constitution will enable it to refer to the Head of State for any institutional issue that may be raised regarding its jurisdiction/resources or for making competition advocacy suggestions would entrench its importance in policy-making; it would increase its role in and legitimacy in giving opinions on legislation, even if these opinions are non-binding, as discussed further below in Section 3.2.4. In addition, it would remove any conflict of interest that may appear to arise within its role of promoting competitive neutrality; as ECA reviews decisions by the government, it should be separated from the Cabinet of Ministers. This separation would also create greater faith for potential investors in ECA's Competitive Neutrality Strategy (see Section 3.2.4). In fact, Chapter 7 of the State's Ownership Policy Document, focusing on competitive neutrality, specifically mentions the importance of granting ECA complete independence for that purpose.[123] Finally, it would also guarantee the impartiality and independence of its employees, as required of independent authorities in Article 216 of the Constitution, and as explained in Section 3.2.2.

In summary, affiliation with the Head of State is the means by which ECA would gain more independence in conformity with the Egyptian Constitution.

Moreover, to further increase ECA's independence, the composition of its Board should be reviewed. According to Article 12 of ECL, ECA's Board is currently composed of:

(1) "A full-time Chairperson with distinguished experience chosen by the Competent Minister.

(2) A Counsellor from the State Council, holding a vice-president rank, to be chosen by the President of the State Council.

[121] The independence of the ECA from the Prime Minister was highlighted by the interviewee from the consumer association and that from the Consumer Protection Agency.

[122] CMA, Vision, values and strategy for the CMA, 2014, paragraph 2.14. Available at: https://assets.publishing.service.gov.uk/media/5a75a4a8e5274a4368298d8e/CMA13_Vision_and_Values_Strategy_document.pdf.

[123] Arab Republic of Egypt, State Ownership Policy Document, June 2022, p. 18. Available (in Arabic) at: https://www.cabinet.gov.eg/conference/pdf/property-policy-document.pdf.

(3) Two representatives of the relevant ministries, nominated by the Competent Minister.

(4) Three specialists with experience in the field of economics and law nominated by the Chairperson of the Authority's Board of Directors.

(5) Three members representing the General Federation of Chambers of Commerce, the Federation of Egyptian Industries, and the General Federation for Consumer Protection, and each Federation/Union shall choose its own representative."

Evidently, the Board, despite the last amendments to Article 12 of ECL in 2014, remains lacking an adequate number of experts in competition law and economics, and comprises a total of five representatives from the business community and the government. It is recommended that the ministerial representation is removed, in order to remove any political considerations from the decision making process. For the same reasons, it would make sense to rethink the participation in the Board of the representatives of the Chamber of Commerce and the Federation of Industries as the opinions of the business community can be taken into account during the investigation stage. Instead, it is suggested that the Board retains the Counsel from the State Council and increases the number of experts (potentially to at least 5). This is similar to the structure of the Saudi Arabian General Authority for Competition[124] as well as the Brazilian Administrative Council for Economic Defence.[125] If, in any case, the Board finds that additional insights are required in the process of making its decision, it can invite any specialist it sees fit, according to Article 13 of ECL, although they will not have the right to vote.

Finally, it should be noted that ECL does not currently explicitly state that decisions of the Board benefit from executive power, which would ensure that matters decided by the Board would not be re-presented in front of the same or different bodies, and that they are enforceable without being re-litigated by an administrative body or court. Explicitly granting this power to ECA's decisions would enhance their authority, as well as re-assert the independence of the Board. This power is also especially relevant for cases in the digital sector, where market changes occur quickly, requiring the quick execution of ECA's decisions. In any case, as explained in the introductory section, ECA's decisions are subject to judicial review from the administrative courts.

In summary, it is suggested that ECL is amended to ensure the independence of ECA, in line with Articles 27, 215 and 216 of the Egyptian Constitution. The composition of its Board should also be reviewed in order to remove any potential political or business influence from its final decisions.

3.2.2. Investigative powers

The first sentence of Article 11 of ECL lays out ECA's power to "[r]eceiv[e] requests for inquiry, investigation, and collection of information, and issu[e] orders to initiate such actions in relation to anti-competitive agreements and practices. This shall be done in accordance with the procedures set out by the Executive Regulations".

To enable ECA to carry out this power, Article 17 of ECL states that "[e]mployees of the Authority, whose appointment shall be declared by the Minister of Justice, in agreement with the Competent Minister and upon the recommendation of the Board, shall be granted the status of Law Enforcement Officers regarding the application of the provisions of this Law. Such employees shall be entitled to review records and documents, as well as to obtain the necessary information and data to examine the cases presented to the Authority from any governmental or non-governmental entity".

As such, Article 23 of LCP, read with the Minister of Justice's Decrees No. 8483 of 2006 and

[124] Article 18 of Saudi Arabian Competition Law (2019).
[125] Article 6 of Law No. 12.529 (2011).

No. 6670 of 2023,[126] together show that employees of ECA with the title of Legal Researcher, Economic Researcher, or Information Technology Specialist, along with the Chairperson, are granted the title of Law Enforcement Officers.

However, these powers differ from the powers of the public prosecution; as mentioned in Section 1.4.1, ECA's officials may collect information rather than investigate, which is something only the prosecution can do. Accordingly, officials at ECA have the following powers, listed in Article 38 of ECLER:

"1. Reviewing records and documents, as well as obtaining any information or data from any governmental or non-governmental authority for the purpose of handling cases submitted to the Authority.

2. Entering, during official working hours, workplaces or headquarters of Persons subject to examination and they may seek assistance from the Public Authority personnel if needed.

3. Carrying out the necessary procedures of collecting information necessary for examination and interrogating any person regarding his committing of any breach of the provisions of the Law."

Granting such powers to officials of ECA is essential for their work, as it allows them to carry out dawn raids when necessary, interview stakeholders, as well as request the data and documents needed to carry out their mandate. Also, dawn raids are carried out following a decision by ECA's Executive Director, and do not require any prior authorization nor notification to any executive or judicial bodies (unless ECA prefers to be accompanied by police forces, in which case it would need to notify them in advance). Moreover, Law Enforcement Officers also, arguably, have the power to inspect the personal premises (following permission from the public prosecution) of those suspected to be involved in anti-competitive behaviour, if it is believed that these premises contain evidence.[127]

Furthermore, there are fines for non-cooperation during dawn raids, not responding to data requests, or providing incorrect data (including in relation to merger control) in Articles 22 bis, 22 b bis, and 22 d bis of ECL. However, there are currently no sanctions for refusing to meet with ECA, meaning that persons can ignore formal invitations from ECA to conduct a meeting or interview. This may result in inefficiencies in the conduct of the interviews necessary to gather evidence or understand the market.

Also imperative to ECA's work and its independence is the mechanism through which investigations are initiated. As stated in Article 11(1) of ECL quoted above, ECA may begin an investigation on its own accord, or following a complaint or request. These are often initiated based on findings established through market monitoring, as discussed in the following sub-section.

Notably, ECA's current investigation powers are in many ways significant, but they could be further strengthened by enhancing the overall independence of ECA, as suggested in Section 3.2.1. Article 216 of the Egyptian Constitution includes the requirement for an independent authority to enjoy "guarantees for its independence and the necessary protection for its employees and the rest of their conditions, to ensure [its] neutrality and independence". Hence, increased independence would improve the effectiveness of the investigation while also protecting ECA employees as they carry out their mandate.

[126] The latter decree replaced the former in 2023. The 2006 decree had generally granted all Legal and Economic Researchers, as well as Information Technology Specialists, the status of Law Enforcement Officers. The 2023 decree instead named the current holders of these titles, granting them this status, as well as granting it to the current Chairperson of ECA.

[127] Mourad Greiss, Investigative powers of the Egyptian Competition Authority: A guide for companies in the Egyptian market, European Competition Law Review, Volume 31, Issue 11, 2010, p. 459-465.

Accordingly, in order to enhance ECA's investigation powers, ECL should be amended to make it mandatory for persons who receive formal request for attendance from ECA to respond to these requests and/or participate in meetings with ECA, otherwise they would face a fine. Additionally, to empower its investigators, ECA should be granted greater independence as per Articles 27, 215, and 216 of the Egyptian Constitution.

3.2.3. Market monitoring

As mentioned previously, one of the powers of ECA, as laid out in Article 11 of ECL, is to create a database of economic activity in Egypt, or in other words, to exert efforts in monitoring the state of competition in different markets. As such, ECA has dedicated resources to this task, initially by the establishment of a Market Monitor Department. The Department, in 2021, became a unit of the newly established Economic Intelligence Department (under the name of the Economic Investigations Unit), which also comprises of the Economic Review Unit and the Databases Unit (see Figure 1).[128] ECA's Strategy 2021-2025 also lists market monitoring as one of the sub-pillars under Pillar 1 on enforcement. Since its creation, ECA has surveyed multiple markets and produced reports encompassing studies and recommendations. These markets include namely the cement, steel, school uniform, pharmaceutical, and dairy markets.[129] An outline of ECA's intervention in the pharmaceutical and school uniforms market is provided below as examples of the extent and limits of ECA's market monitoring powers.

Box 3

ECA's market monitoring efforts in the pharmaceutical and school uniform markets

Pharmaceuticals

In 2023, ECA began the process of setting up a database of the pharmaceutical market, in order to aid its efforts in this priority sector. The project proceeded in the following steps:

(1) Preparing a policy paper on defining markets in the pharmaceutical sector.
(2) Creating a database to include:
   a. The main elements of the licensed/producing undertakings are the pharmaceutical product's name and dosage, the active pharmaceutical ingredient, and its therapeutic class.
   b. Quantitative data, such as quantities sold and the selling prices for producers and distribution companies.

The database currently includes the following information for each pharmaceutical product:

(1) Name of licensed company.
(2) Name of producing company.
(3) Name of pharmaceutical product.
(4) Source of pharmaceutical product (imported/local).
(5) Dosage of pharmaceutical, according to new form code (NFC) classification.

[128] Information obtained from ECA.

[129] World Bank Group, Changing Mindsets to Transform Markets: Lessons Learned from the First Annual Awards in Competition Policy Advocacy, 2014. Available at: https://documents1.worldbank.org/curated/en/609211474266532681/pdf/108251-WP-Competition-Policy-Awards-PUBLIC.pdf; and ECA's Annual Reports 2015-2021. Available (in Arabic) here.

(6) Substitutable pharmaceutical products according to anatomical therapeutic chemical (ATC) classification.

(7) The pharmaceutical product's active pharmaceutical ingredient (API).

School uniforms

Up to 2014, ECA received multiple complaints from the parents of schoolchildren regarding the prices and quality of school uniforms. Upon investigation, ECA found that one of the main reasons for the deteriorating quality and the rising prices of the uniforms was the fact that schools entered into *de facto* exclusivity agreements with suppliers.[130] As such, ECA cooperated with the Ministry of Education to issue a joint circular to all schools, instructing them to not carry out such practices, and laying out that an administrative fine might be applied in cases of non-compliance.[131]

In 2022 and 2023, ECA again received complaints regarding exclusivity in selling school uniforms. Upon investigating these complaints, it issued infringement decisions against four schools, namely for infringing Articles 7 and 8 of ECL. ECA had established that each school constructed a relevant market for its consumers, students, who were locked into that market once they had enrolled in the school.[132]

Meanwhile, ECA launched a full-scale investigation into the sector, using, for the first time since its creation, an online survey. Two hundred and eighty schools in the cities of Cairo and Giza responded to this survey, representing a total of 326,240 students from different types of schools: public, private, and international. Using this information, ECA was able to identify the most common types of anti-competitive practices in the school uniform sector, and accordingly issue guidance for schools and suppliers alike on how to avoid ECA infringements.[133] Following the publication of the guidelines,[134] at the start of the 2023/2024 school year, ECA received more complaints against schools, raising the number of prohibited uncovered conduct to amount to 15 schools by the end of 2023. During this time, ECA again cooperated with the Ministry of Education, which issued Decree No. 167 of 2023, reiterating many of the recommendations made by ECA in the School Uniform Guidelines. This example serves as a successful instance of market monitoring, detection, and intervention by ECA.

As illustrated above, once ECA carries out a market study, its powers are limited to either: (1) pursuing specific anti-competitive infringements, (2) issuing non-binding guidelines targeting the market players involved, or (3) making recommendations to amend state-measures, if appropriate, under Article 11/5 of ECL (see Section 3.2.4). Unlike some jurisdictions, such as

[130] World Bank Group, Changing Mindsets to Transform Markets: Lessons Learned from the First Annual Awards in Competition Policy Advocacy, 2014, p. 37. Available at: https://documents1.worldbank.org/curated/en/609211474266532681/pdf/108251-WP-Competition-Policy-Awards-PUBLIC.pdf.

[131] Decree of Minister of Education No 420 of 2014.

[132] Nicolas Bremer, Egyptian Competition Authority (ECA) Conducts Investigation into the Market for School Uniforms, 2023. Available at: https://www.bremerlf.com/resources/egyptian-competition-authority-eca-conducts-investigation-into-the-market-for-school-uniforms-2?utm_source=mondaq&utm_medium=syndication&utm_term=Anti-trustCompetition-Law&utm_content=articleoriginal&utm_campaign=article.

[133] The Competition Authority Continues to Address Infringements Regarding School Uniforms, 20 January 2022. Available (in Arabic) here.

[134] ECA's School Uniform Guidelines, 2023. Available at: https://awards.concurrences.com/IMG/pdf/eca_school_uniform_guidelines.pdf?117404/0cca55748688c057f6a9ad08c83ea4435119a8f61db81ac4d46bd217d9df3f93.

Spain,[135] Mexico,[136] Greece[137] and the United Kingdom Market Investigation Regime, ECA is unable to issue remedies, which may improve the competition landscape in a market or pre-emptively halt competitive behaviour from taking place. While ECA was indeed able to issue such an administrative decision in 2014, this was through its cooperation with the Ministry of Education, and not on its own accord.

Having the power to impose remedies, structural or behavioural, following a market study, would allow ECA to address anti-competitive structures or conduct across the specific industry that may not always be adequately pursued under the current provisions of ECL. For instance, remedies could be imposed on players in oligopolistic markets in which tacit collusion is likely, following the existence of some facilitating practices which do not fall by themselves within the scope of the anti-trust provisions of ECL. The same applies to "new" markets, such as digital markets which often "tip" in favour of a market player. Having the ability to impose remedies, even prophylactic ones, in such markets could prevent the exclusion of potential competitors and possible mavericks.[138]

In conclusion, it becomes apparent that while ECA currently employs the capacity and resources to carry out market investigations, which have in the past proven successful, it lacks the power to impose remedies in order to promote competition in the markets studied. This power should be considered, given how it would support efforts to protect competition in oligopolistic or nascent markets.

3.2.4. Limiting anti-competitive state measures and promoting competitive neutrality

Since its creation, ECA has dedicated resources to advocacy efforts, namely those laid out in Article 11(5) of ECL, which allows ECA to issue its opinion regarding legislations, policies, or decrees that may affect competition, and obliges concerned government authorities to consult ECA on such measures. As mentioned in the previous sub-Section, ECA's opinion is often based on a market study, or it could be issued upon a request from any state entity to review draft or existing legislation. Since 2013, ECA has issued 96 opinions on state measures of different forms.[139] Of particular interest is also the cooperation between ECA and the Consumer Protection Agency, in particular with regard to government initiatives imposing price caps ("maximum prices") for certain categories of strategic products.[140]

---

[135] Since 2013, the National Commission of Markets and Competition has the power to challenge before the Courts Public Administration's legal actions and general provisions hierarchically inferior to law that hinder the maintenance of effective competition in the markets (Article 5.4 of Law 3/2013).

[136] Article 94 of the Federal Law of Economic Competition which empowers the Federal Economic Competition Commission to determine (1) the existence of barriers to competition and free market access, or (2) of an essential facility in a specific market, to impose behavioural and structural remedies and to issue recommendations to authorities of any level of government to eliminate regulatory barriers identified in a market investigation.

[137] Article 11 of Law 3959/2011.

[138] Massimo Motta et al., Market Investigations in the EU, in Massimo Motta et al. (ed), Market Investigations: A New Competition Tool for Europe, Cambridge University Press 2021, p. 3.

[139] Data obtained from ECA.

[140] In his interview, the consumer protection official emphasized the importance of cooperation between ECA and the Consumer Protection Agency, with regard to the imposition of price caps (maximum price) for certain strategic products (packed mixed oils beans, rice, milk, white sugar, pasta and white cheese) starting from 1 March 2024 following the Minister Council Decision No. 5000 of 2023 and Ministry of Supply and Internal Trade Decision No. 200 of 2023. The New Regulations will enter into force for six months, subject to renewal and any infringement, such as the withholding or refusal to deal conducts related to any of the strategic goods, in the supply and/or distribution chain will be punished according to the provisions of Consumer Law Protection Law No. 181 of 2018.

The 2021-2025 Strategy clarifies in Pilar 2 that one of ECA's key focuses is limiting anti-competitive state measures and promoting competitive neutrality. Based on this pillar, in 2022, ECA developed its Competitive Neutrality Strategy. This has been approved and supported by the Cabinet of Ministers, as evidenced by the text of Chapter 7 of the State Ownership Policy Document, which points out the importance of promoting competitive neutrality and ECA's pivotal role in fulfilling this goal.[141]

ECA's Competitive Neutrality Strategy comprises of four pillars:

(1) Setting the institutional framework.

(2) Setting the regulatory framework.

(3) Raising awareness of competitive neutrality.

(4) Carrying out periodic ex-post assessment.

Publishing the Competitive Neutrality Strategy was an important development towards creating an open environment for investments.[142]

The institutional framework entailed creating ECA's Competition Policy and Competitive Neutrality (CPCN) Department, which has been active since September 2022. The CPCN Department receives complaints and initiates studies into new and existing state measures which potentially harm competition and competitive neutrality; namely those that facilitate collusion, raise barriers to entry and expansion, and/or discriminate between market players based on their nationality or ownership. The CPCN Department then raises its findings to the High Committee on Competition Policy and Competitive Neutrality.

This Committee was created in June 2022 through Prime Ministerial Decision No. 2195 of 2022. It is headed by the Prime Ministers and its members are a number of Ministers as well as Heads and representatives of government authorities, with ECA being the technical rapporteur or the technical secretariat of the Committee.

The Committee reviews state measures to ensure that they are not anti-competitive and do not distort competitive neutrality, drawing on the technical studies carried out by ECA (CPCN Department). The Committee may amend or repeal anti-competitive state measures. Its decisions are binding to all administrative authorities. In the past, it has made decisions covering a variety of sectors, including petroleum, healthcare and food production.

Moreover, one of the recent projects of the CPCN Department, in cooperation with ECA's Bid-Rigging Department, was to review the purchasing guidelines of state authorities. These guidelines essentially lay out the specific procurement rules for each authority, and can in themselves facilitate collusion, create artificial barriers to entry, or discriminate between different types of undertakings. ECA has, in 2023, reviewed and issued recommendations regarding five purchasing guidelines.

The substantive analysis of state measures is explained in ECA's Guidelines for Assessing the Impact of State Measures on Competition.[143] Drafted in cooperation with the World Bank Group, the Guidelines lay out ECA's process in analysing state measures, such as market definition, the analysis of the impact of the state measure in question on competition, any justifications regarding its effect on competition, and accordingly explores less restrictive regulatory alternatives. The Guidelines have also been disseminated amongst public entities through a circular issued by the

[141] Arab Republic of Egypt, State Ownership Policy Document, June 2022, p. 18. Available (in Arabic) at: https://www.cabinet.gov.eg/conference/pdf/property-policy-document.pdf.

[142] Notably ECA was one of the winners in the 2023 ICN advocacy contest for its efforts in the area of competitive neutrality: see https://www.worldbank.org/en/events/2023/05/22/competition-advocacy-contest-2023.

[143] ECA, Guidelines for Assessing the Impact of State Measures on Competition, 2022. Available at: https://awards.concurrences.com/IMG/pdf/competition_impact_assessment_of_state_measures.pdf.

Prime Minister, encouraging decision makers to consider them when drafting state measures, and to consult ECA's opinion in accordance with Article 11(5) of ECL. Additionally, in 2023, Law No. 195 of 2023 was issued, removing any preferential treatment provided to state-owned enterprises, specifically with regard to taxes or fees.

In terms of raising awareness on the concept of competitive neutrality, ECA has focused on explaining the concept of competitive neutrality and bid-rigging (see Section 3.2.7) to the employees of different public entities across Egypt. Around 40 workshops have been hosted in different cities since 2021.[144]

Finally, ECA is currently developing a Competitive Neutrality Index with the aim of measuring perceived competitive neutrality in different sectors in a quantitative manner. The Index utilizes a survey, sent to all market players in a number of sectors, and results are compared across several years, in order to highlight the competitive neutrality issues in different markets. In addition, the Index will also assist ECA to assess the effectiveness of its interventions in different markets, by comparing results of post-intervention to those expected *ex-ante*.

While ECA has undertaken strides in the area of preventing anti-competitive state measures, recommendations under Article 11(5) of ECL remain non-binding; state entities are obliged to consult ECA on state measures affecting competition, but ECA's opinion is not binding on them, while the decisions of the High Committee are binding.

ECA's efforts in the area of promoting competitive neutrality should be supported by amendments to ECL which allow it to issue binding opinions, especially given the state's expressed intention to promote competitive neutrality. These amendments may include a mechanism under which state institutions, in case they diverge from ECA's recommendations, issue a memo explaining their reasons for divergence. This would also enable individuals and undertakings to challenge anti-competitive legislation in court, similar to what was observed in the 1953 case explained in Section 1.2.

3.2.5. International relations and regional cooperation

Article 11(6) of ECL lists cooperation with international jurisdictions as one of ECA's competences, and ECA has identified this as one of its goals under Pillar 1.6 of its Strategy 2021-2025. ECA's involvement in the international competition community mainly takes three forms: involvement in international networks and events, cooperation with other competition authorities and organizations, and participation in regional and international initiatives and agreements.

ECA has been an active member of the International Competition Network (ICN) and the OECD Competition Committee, as well as UNCTAD's Intergovernmental Group of Experts (IGE) on Competition Law and Policy,[145] contributing to conferences and workshops through written contributions and presentations. It has also participated in other conferences held by UNCTAD and UN-ESCWA.[146] In recent years, ECA has made contributions mainly on the topics of digital

[144] Data obtained from ECA.

[145] For instance, ECA presented its Strategy for the Years 2021-2025 and its recent achievements, particularly relating to promoting competitive neutrality, at the UNCTAD's 21st Session of the IGE on Competition Law and Policy held in Geneva, Switzerland. See ECA, ECA Participates in Meetings of the Intergovernmental Group of Experts Held by the UNCTAD in Switzerland and Presents Achievements on Advocacy and Competitive Neutrality, 16 July 2023. Available (in Arabic) here.

[146] OECD, in cooperation with UNCTAD and UN-ESCWA, has, since 2019, held an annual conference for the MENA Region (The Arab Competition Forum). ECA is an active participant in these conferences. For more information, see https://www.oecd.org/daf/competition/middle-east-north-africa-competition-forum.htm.

markets,[147] sector regulation,[148] and sustainability,[149] among others. Its more general contributions are the Annual Reports submitted to OECD[150] and the ICN's Cartel Enforcement Template.[151] Moreover, ECA became a co-chair of the ICN's Advocacy Working Group in 2023.[152] Notably, in 2018, ECA and UNCTAD launched the Regional Training Centre for Competition, aimed at providing workshops for competition officials in the Middle East and North Africa.[153] The mandate of the Training Centre was later amended to include the whole of Africa. ECA has since worked on assembling an Advisory Board for the centre.[154]

In terms of regional cooperation, ECA has played a leading role in both the Middle Eastern and African regions. In 2022, ECA launched the Arab Competition Network (ACN), bringing together all Arab states in the Greater Arab Free Trade Area with the aim of promoting cooperation and coordination, as well as supporting states looking to employ or strengthen their competition law and policy.[155] The ACN comprises of three working groups focused on: agency effectiveness, enforcement, and merger control. It is headed by ECA for the period of 2022-2024. In addition to the initial launch event in Cairo, Egypt in March 2022, the second conference was held in March 2023 in Morocco.[156] The ACN also initiated and hosted two editions of the Arab Competition Authority Simulation (Arab CAS), which offers law and students of economics the opportunity to attend presentations on different competition-related topics by anti-trust officials, as well as solve a real-life case.[157] It is modelled after an initiative launched by ECA more than a decade ago and held annually, under the same name. The working groups of the ACN meet, remotely, year-round to exchange experiences and expertise.

ECA also plays a prominent role in the African region. In 2016, it signed a MoU with the COMESA Competition Commission, with the purpose of facilitating coordination and harmonizing competition laws and policies.[158] ECA often participates in conferences and workshops held by the COMESA. For instance, ECA recently hosted the COMESA Competition Commission's

[147] See, for example, Merger Control in Dynamic Markets - Contribution from Egypt, 2019. Available at: https://one.oecd.org/document/DAF/COMP/GF/WD(2019)22/en/pdf; Start-ups, killer acquisitions and merger control - Note by Egypt, 2020. Available at: https://one.oecd.org/document/DAF/COMP/WD(2020)26/en/pdf; and ICN MENA Region Working Group Report on Merger Control in Times of Crisis, 2020. Available at: https://www.internationalcompetitionnetwork.org/wp-content/uploads/2022/04/MWG_Webinar-Merger-Control-Covid_MENA_2020.pdf (project led by ECA).

[148] Interactions Between Competition Authorities and Sector Regulators - Contribution from Egypt, 2022. Available at: https://one.oecd.org/document/DAF/COMP/GF/WD(2022)10/en/pdf.

[149] Competition in the Circular Economy - Note by Egypt, 2023. Available at: https://one.oecd.org/document/DAF/COMP/WD(2023)43/en/pdf#:~:text=circular%20economy%20encompasses%20three%20key,considerations%20into%20its%20competition%20assessments.

[150] OECD, Annual Reports by Competition Agencies on recent developments. Available at: https://www.oecd.org/competition/annualreportsbycompetitionagencies.htm.

[151] Egyptian Competition Authority, ICN Anti-cartel Enforcement Template. Available at: https://www.internationalcompetitionnetwork.org/wp-content/uploads/2023/06/CWG_Template_Egypt-2022.pdf.

[152] International Competition Network, The Mission of the Advocacy Working Group (AWG). Available at: https://www.internationalcompetitionnetwork.org/working-groups/advocacy/.

[153] UNCTAD, Cairo home to new competition-focused training centre, 21 November 2018. Available at: https://unctad.org/news/cairo-home-new-competition-focused-training-centre.

[154] Information obtained from ECA.

[155] Arab Competition Network, Protocol on cooperation in the field of competition among Arab Countries, Cooperation protocol, 16 March 2022. Available (in Arabic) at: https://arabcompetitionnetwork.com/law-and-protocol/.

[156] ECA, With Egyptian Leadership and Morocco Hosting, the Launch of the Second Annual ACN Conference, 11 March 2023. Available (in Arabic) here.

[157] ECA, Conclusion of First Edition of the Arab Competition Authority Simulation, Winners Granted Opportunity to Attend Meeting of the Arab Competition Network, 08 February 2023. Available (in Arabic) here.

[158] Cooperation Agreement Framework Between the COMESA Competition Commission and the Egyptian Competition Authority Regarding Cooperation in the Application and Enforcement of the COMESA Competition Regulations, August 2016. Available at: https://www.comesacompetition.org/wp-content/uploads/2016/08/Cooperation-Framework-Agreements-ECA-and-CCC.pdf.

annual meeting in September 2023.[159] ECA's Chairperson, Dr. Mahmoud Momtaz, has served as a Commissioner to its Board since 2021.[160] Furthermore, as mentioned in Section 2.1.4, ECA has reviewed 151 cases referred to it by the COMESA Competition Commission, highlighting the success of their cooperation.

Moreover, in February 2022, ECA, along with the competition authorities of Kenya, Mauritius, Nigeria, and South Africa issued a statement, launching the Africa Heads of Competition Dialogue. In February 2023, the heads of these authorities, as well as those of the COMESA Competition Commission and the competition authorities in Gambia, Morocco, and Zambia met again in Cairo, Egypt, and agreed on setting a working group tasked with generally collaborating on issues relating to digital markets and enhancing capacity building.[161] Notably, throughout 2022 and 2023, ECA played a key role in the negotiation of the African Continental Free Trade Area agreements, namely in the discussions relating to the Protocol on Competition Policy.[162]

In terms of bilateral agreements, ECA has signed a total of 15 bilateral protocols and MoUs with competition authorities from different jurisdictions, the most recent of which are with the Hellenic Competition Authority, the Commission for the Protection of Competition of the Republic of Cyprus, and the Competition Commission of India.[163] Notably, between the period of January 2015 and April 2017, ECA benefitted from a twinning programme with both the Federal Ministry for Economic Affairs and Energy of Germany and the Competition Council of the Republic of Lithuania.[164] ECA has indeed, in practice, benefitted from cooperating with other competition authorities, including on an *ad hoc* basis, in specific investigations. An example of this is the Uber/Careem merger.

Box 4

Cooperation between ECA and other competition authorities in the case of Uber/Careem[165]

In 2019, ECA carried out an assessment of the acquisition of global ride-hailing company Uber of its regional counterpart, Careem. The acquisition was to take place in several jurisdictions, including Saudi Arabia and Pakistan. During its investigation, Egypt invited the Saudi Arabian General Authority for Competition, the Competition Commission of Pakistan, and the COMESA Competition Commission to hold bilateral meetings in order to exchange opinions and conclusions regarding the assessment (under confidential waivers signed by the undertakings in question). Accordingly, the four entities were able to issue similar decisions, ultimately allowing the transaction with remedies (for the Egyptian regime, this was done under Article 6(2) of ECL). This cooperation was associated with a number of benefits, such as building expertise in the area of merger control in digital markets and coordinating actions in a manner that creates optimal outcomes for all markets involved.

[159] ECA, ECA Hosts Meetings of COMESA Competition Commission, 17 September 2023. Available at: https://www.sis.gov.eg/Story/185816/Egypt-hosts-meetings-of-COMESA-Competition-Commission?lang=en-us.

[160] See https://comesacompetition.org/board_member/mahmoud-a-momtaz/.

[161] Africa Heads of Competition Dialogue, Joint Statement of the African Heads of Competition Authorities Dialogue on Regulation of Digital Markets, 08 February 2023. Available at: https://comesacompetition.org/wp-content/uploads/2023/02/Joint-Statement-of-the-Africa-Heads-of-Competition-Dialogue-08-Feb-2023-Cairo83561.pdf.

[162] Information obtained from ECA.

[163] Information obtained from ECA.

[164] Competition Council of the Republic of Lithuania, Twinning Project in Egypt. Available at: https://kt.gov.lt/en/about-us/international-cooperation/twinning-project-in-egypt.

[165] ECA, ECA's Assessment of the Acquisition of Careem, Inc. by Uber Technologies Inc., 2019. Available at: https://www.docdroid.net/GXSIQ7c/ecas-assessment-of-the-acquisition-of-careem-inc-by-uber-technologies-incnon-confidential1-pdf.

Evidently, ECA has placed a large focus on international cooperation, placing it in a leading role in the regions of Africa and the Middle East, and resulting in benefits on several technical and procedural fronts.

3.2.6. Agency resources

This Section discusses ECA's human and financial resources, exploring how they compare to those of other competition authorities, and whether or not they are adequate in empowering ECA to carry out its role, especially noting ECA's enforcement record, as discussed in the following Section.

Figure 1 displays ECA's budget[166] for every fiscal year[167] since 2006 (in EGP).

Figure 1
ECA's Budget per Fiscal Year (2006-2023)

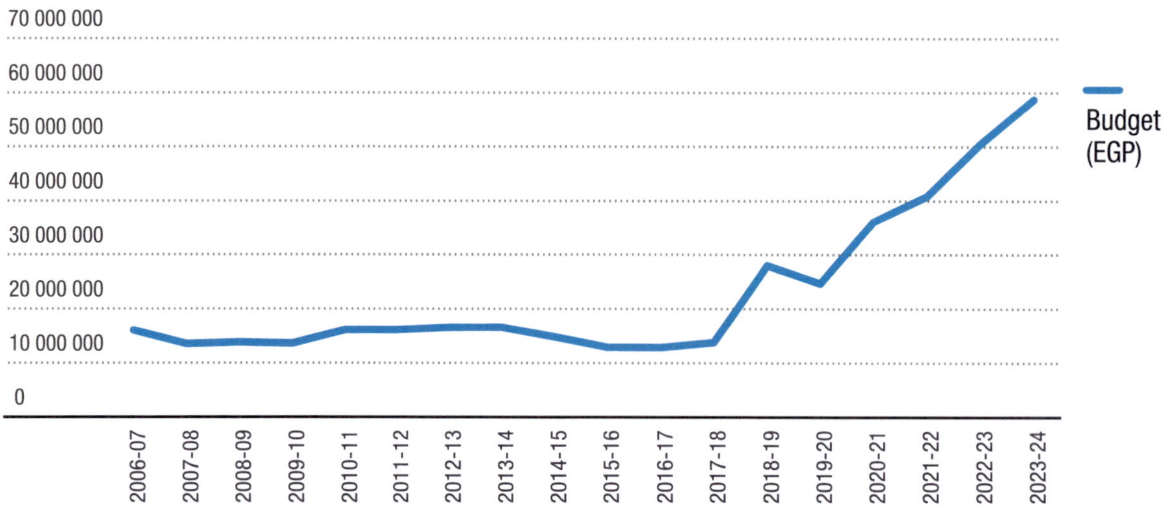

Figure 2 compares the budget to that of the average of OECD, non-OECD, and Middle Eastern and African competition authorities (in EUR), as reported to OECD for the years 2015-2022.[168]

[166] These values were obtained from ECA. They represent the main source of ECA's budget, i.e. that allocated from Parliament (as in Article 14(1) of ECL).
[167] The Egyptian fiscal year begins on July 1 and ends on June 30 of each year.
[168] ECA's budget has been converted to Euros using the average exchange rate for each fiscal year, respectively. Each Egyptian fiscal year is compared to the calendar which corresponds to its first half (i.e. 2015-2016 is compared to 2015). The OECD data is downloaded from: https://www.oecd.org/competition/oecd-competition-trends.htm.

Figure 2
ECA's Budget Compared to Global Averages (2015-2022)

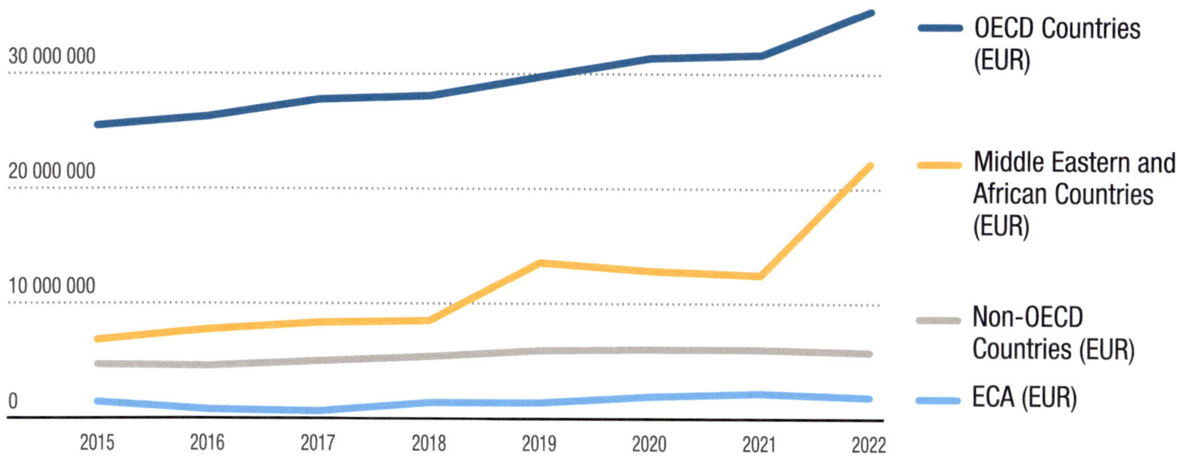

It is evident from these two Figures that ECA's budget, on average, sits below that of other Middle Eastern and African competition authorities, as well as other non-OECD competition authorities. Naturally, one of the key expenditures of an institution is its human resources, in terms of hiring and building capacity. Figure 3 shows the number of total staff employed by ECA from 2006-2023.

Figure 3
Total Number of Staff

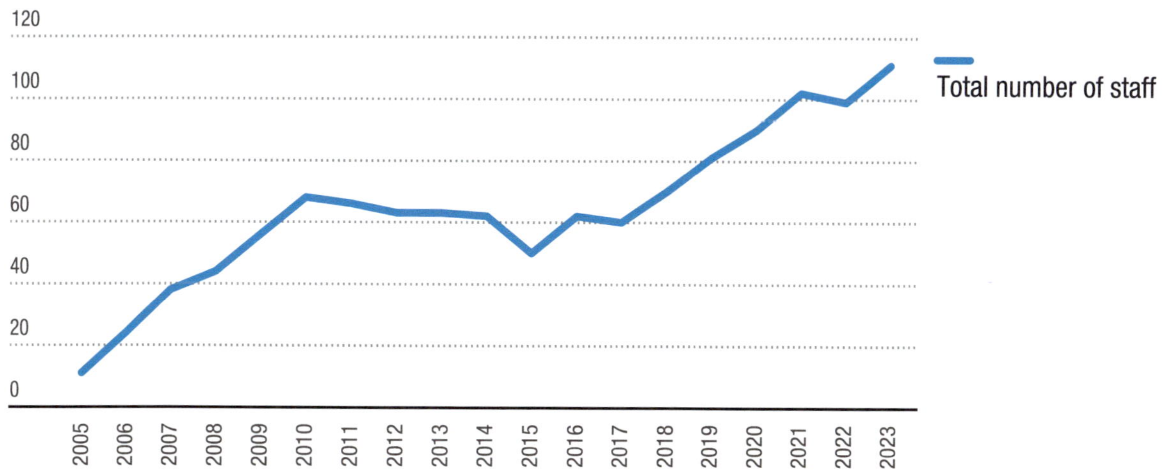

While the number of staff has increased, it also becomes apparent from Figure 4 that ECA's total workload has increased over time, in terms of complaints, initiations, leniency applications, requests for exemption from Article 6 and from Article 9 of ECL, market studies, and merger notifications in the healthcare sector (see Section 2.1.4).

Figure 4
Total Number of Cases

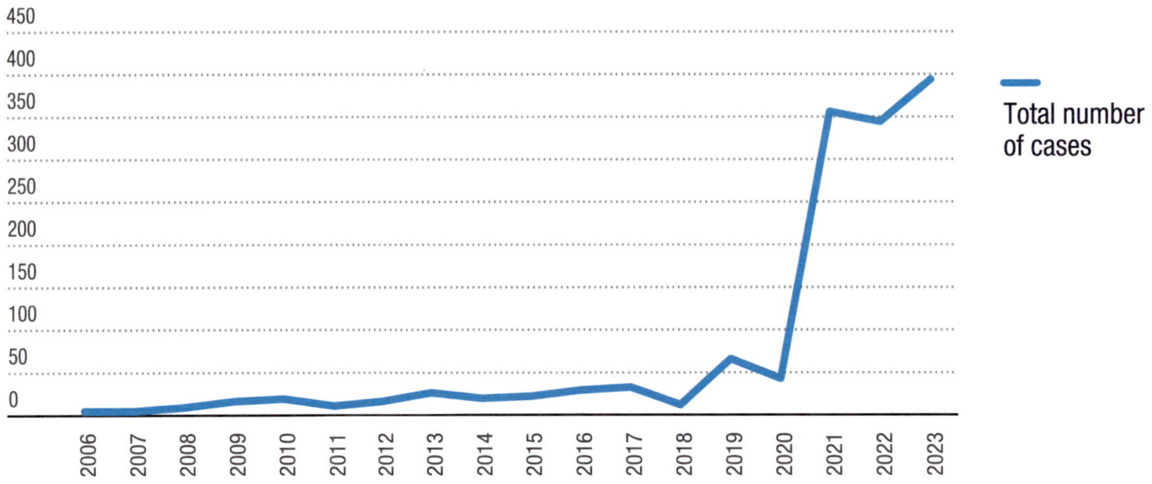

This underscores the need for more budgetary and human resources. This need is also exemplified by comparing the number of staff members of ECA to those in other jurisdictions. Figure 5 compares the number of competition staff to that of competition authorities in OECD, non-OECD, and Middle Eastern and African competition authorities, as reported to the OECD for the years 2015-2022.[169]

Figure 5
Number of Competition Staff at ECA Compared to Global Averages (2015-2022)

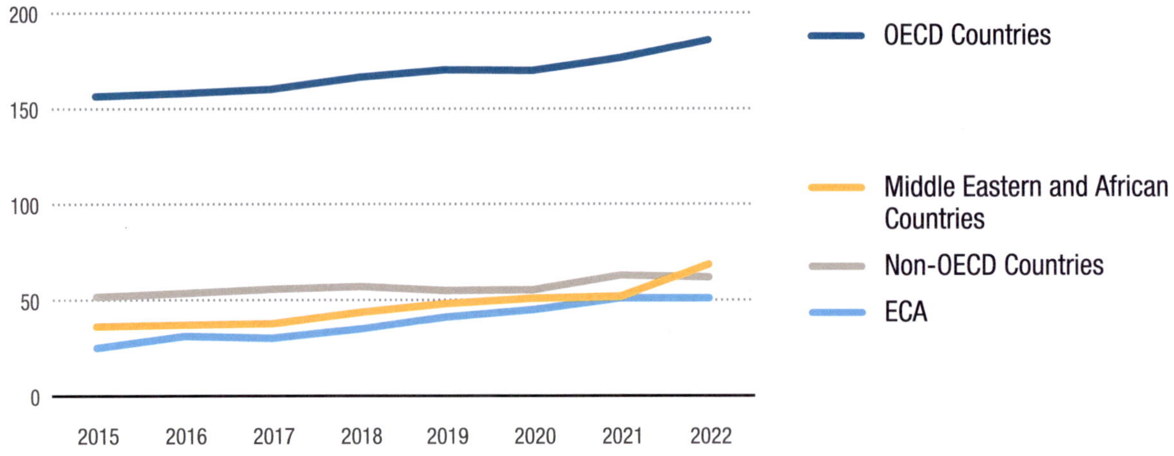

While the number of technical and support staff at ECA has increased over time, the number of competition staff is low compared to other countries, including those in the region. This highlights the importance of considering increasing ECA's budget to allow it to attract and retain a higher number of technical staff. This can be further assured by removing the maximum wage limit

[169] The exact number of competition staff for each year is not available, but it is estimated by ECA that the number of competition staff usually comprised of 50 per cent of the total, so this is the assumption used. The OECD data is downloaded from this link: https://www.oecd.org/competition/oecd-competition-trends.htm.

imposed by Law No. 63 of 2014 regarding the Maximum Wages of Employees of the State, allowing ECA to attract qualified competition experts.[170] This is necessary given the higher salaries in the private sector, as well as the scarcity of such candidates, as competition law is currently taught at few universities in Egypt.

Moreover, it is apparent that ECA could benefit from an internal prioritization mechanism, which does not contravene ECL, in order to ensure efficient use of its scarce resources. While ECA's Strategy 2021-2025 sets out its general priorities for the period, there is no mechanism through which complaints, for instance, are prioritized internally. Competition authorities in other jurisdictions such as United Kingdom CMA,[171] the Swedish Konkurrensverket[172] and the Hellenic Competition Commission[173] have published guidelines on how they use weighting factors or points systems to prioritize cases. Some of the factors these authorities consider include: the nature of the alleged restriction of competition (cartel, abuse of dominance, vertical restriction), whether or not large groups of consumers are harmed by the conduct, the impact of the specific economic sector or markets on the consumer price index, how substantial the impact of the intervention will be, the extent to which the case will cause a deterrent effect, the available resources, the availability of evidence, the novelty of the competition issues raised, and the possible risks of intervention.

In terms of raising capacity, Pillar 4 of ECA's Strategy 2021-2025 makes explicit the ambition to increase the skills of ECA's employees. Several technical experts at ECA have, during their time at ECA, undertaken postgraduate diplomas and master's degrees in the areas of competition law and economics at United States and European universities. In 2022, a member of staff was seconded to the OECD's Competition Division, and in 2023, three members of staff were seconded to the COMESA Competition Commission. Other training provided by ECA, for technical and support staff alike, covered soft skills such as presentation and managerial skills.

From the above, it can be concluded that ECA's budget and number of technical staff are low compared to global averages. Accordingly, its budget should be increased and the wage limit should be removed, especially given the analysis below of ECA's enforcement record.

3.2.7. Enforcement record

Pillar 1 of ECA's Strategy 2021-2025 focuses on its enforcement priorities. For instance, Pillar 1.2 lays out the goals of publishing guidelines on substantive and procedural guidelines, in order to increase efficiency in case-handling, and on focusing on bid-rigging. Regarding the former, ECA updated and re-published its Compliance Toolkit in 2021.[174] In 2023, it published two sets of draft guidelines on public consultation: the Market Definition Guidelines and the Dominance Guidelines. It also recently updated its Frequently Asked Questions document, providing clearer and more updated answers to common queries by consumers and businesses.[175] As mentioned above, ECA also published sector-specific guidelines, relating to the school uniform sector, in the same year. In previous years, ECA had also published guidelines on its leniency policy[176]

[170] It is to be noted that all interviewees highlighted the technocratic competence and high-level expertise of ECA's staff.

[171] CMA, Prioritisation Principles, 2023. Available at: https://assets.publishing.service.gov.uk/media/653f71b780884d0013f71cf4/CMA_Prioritisation_Principles__.pdf.

[172] Konkurrensverket, The Swedish Competition Authority's Prioritisation Policy for Competition Law Enforcement and Supervision of the Public Procurement Rules, 2022. Available at: https://www.konkurrensverket.se/globalassets/dokument/engelska-dokument/english_prioritisation-policy-for-competition-and-public-procurement.pdf.

[173] HCC, Decision 696/2019. Available at: https://www.epant.gr/en/decisions/item/1186-decision-696-2019.html.

[174] ECA, Compliance Toolkit, 2021. Available (in Arabic) here.

[175] Available (in Arabic) here.

[176] ECA, Leniency Guidelines, 2020. Available (in Arabic) here.

and on detecting and avoiding bid-rigging.[177] However, interviews with stakeholders highlighted further need for ECA to communicate to a wider public the benefits of competitive markets and to diffuse information on business conduct that may violate the law, through the publication of guidelines for small and medium enterprises (SMEs), consumers and farmers, but also through more extensive and systematic contacts with the specialized but also general media about the enforcement activities of the authority with the aim to increase awareness about the law and deterrence[178] (beyond the current efforts of publishing press releases, conducting media interviews, and publishing local and international reports). The role of consumer associations and consumers complaints to ECA also needs to be enhanced.[179] Finally, ECA should make efforts through its collaboration with business associations, as well as the publication of guidelines, to enhance the compliance efforts undertaken by businesses.[180]

In the area of bid-rigging, ECA created a dedicated Bid-Rigging Department in 2022. ECA has indeed issued a number of decisions regarding Article 6(c) of ECL in the last period in several sectors such as food and beverage,[181] schoolbooks,[182] vehicle spare parts,[183] lampposts,[184] iron pipes,[185] and chemical products,[186] As mentioned previously, it also cooperated with several government institutes to amend their procurement practices, ensuring that they do not facilitate collusion or distort competitive neutrality. ECA also made presentations in around 40 workshops at different government institutions, explaining how to detect bid-rigging and report it to ECA.

In line with the remainder of the goals of Pillar 1, ECA issued a total of 34 infringement decisions in 2023. Figure 6 shows that this is an increase from previous years, and Figure 7 shows the overall increase in the number of investigations (split into the triggers listed in Article 11 of ECL, i.e. complaints received from natural and juristic persons, requests received from state institutions, and initiations by ECA), while Figure 8 shows the breakdown of decisions by industry.

177 ECA, Bid-Rigging Guidelines, 2021. Available (in Arabic) here.

178 The need for more systematic contacts with specialized and generalist media, in particular the press, was highlighted by the interviewee from the consumer association who noted that competition law "is not engrained in society" and that there is still some lack of awareness about competition law in the general public, but also among small and medium firms.

179 The interviewee from the consumer association highlighted the importance of the possibility of formal complaints by consumers to ECA, in particular noting the contribution of consumer complaints in the school uniform cases. The representative of the Investment Authority highlighted the impact of significant decisions of ECA, such as the cement investigation between 2005-2007 and the hefty fines imposed to each of the cement companies that participated to the infringement, but also the steel investigation, to raise awareness about the new competition law legislation among large business. However, it was noted by some of the interviewees that there is more awareness about the law among large multinational companies and not sufficient awareness among local small and medium firms. One of the highlights of the interviews was the significant efforts made recently to raise awareness about the role of the competition authority and to enhance regulatory compliance, even if significant progress still remains to be made.

180 Interview with a representative of the main business association and an official of the investment authority.

181 ECA, ECA Proves Violation of Several Associations for Colluding Regarding Selling School Meals in the Governorate of Minya, 08 January 2024. Available (in Arabic) here.

182 ECA, ECA Proves the Violation of 33 Printing Companies Regarding Printing and Providing Books to the Ministry of Education, 04 January 2024. Available (in Arabic) here.

183 ECA, As a Part of it's Goal to Prosecute Bid-Rigging in Public Procurement… ECA Proves Violation of Two Providers of Spare Parts to the Cairo Transport Authority, 21 May 2023. Available (in Arabic) here.

184 ECA, As a Part of it's Goal to Prosecute Bid-Rigging in Public Procurement… ECA Proves Violation Companies in the Markets for Lamp Posts and Iron Pipes, 30 January 2023. Available (in Arabic) here.

185 Ibid.

186 ECA, Achievements of ECA in 2022, 31 December 2022. Available (in Arabic) here.

Figure 6
Infringement Decisions (2006-2023)

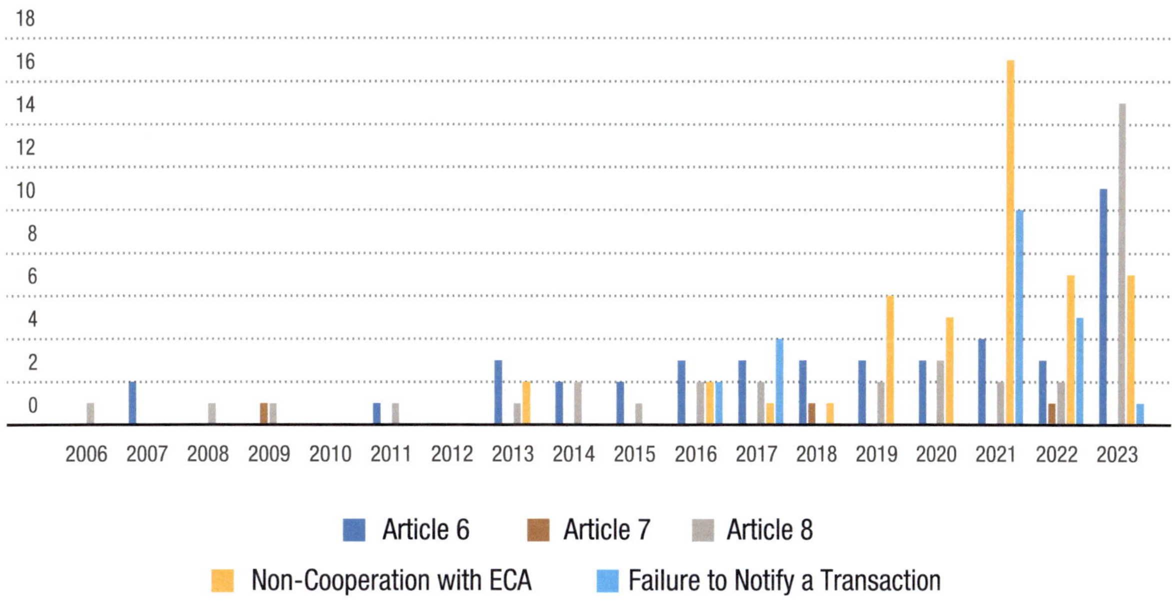

Figure 7
ECA Cases by Type of Trigger (2006-2023)

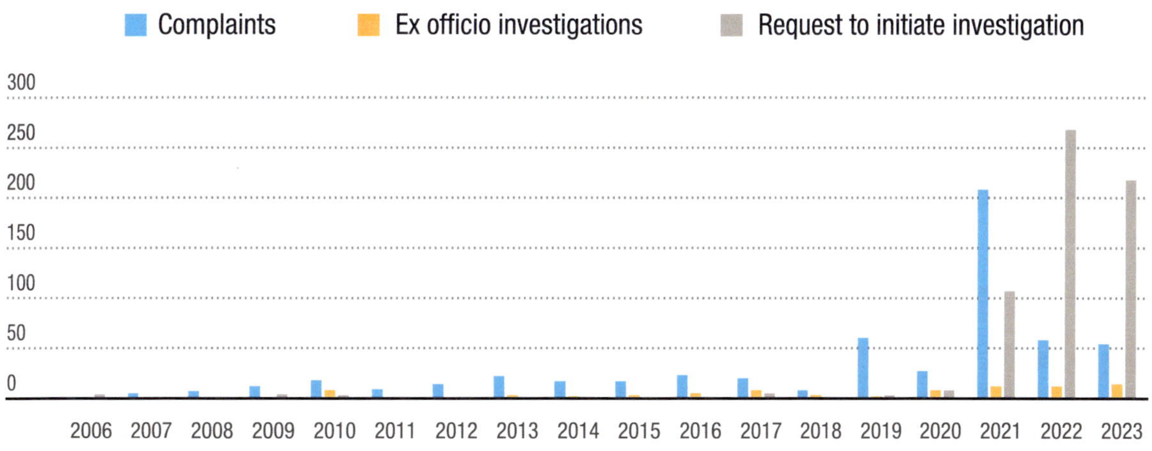

Figure 8

Article 6-8 Decisions By Sector (2018-2023)

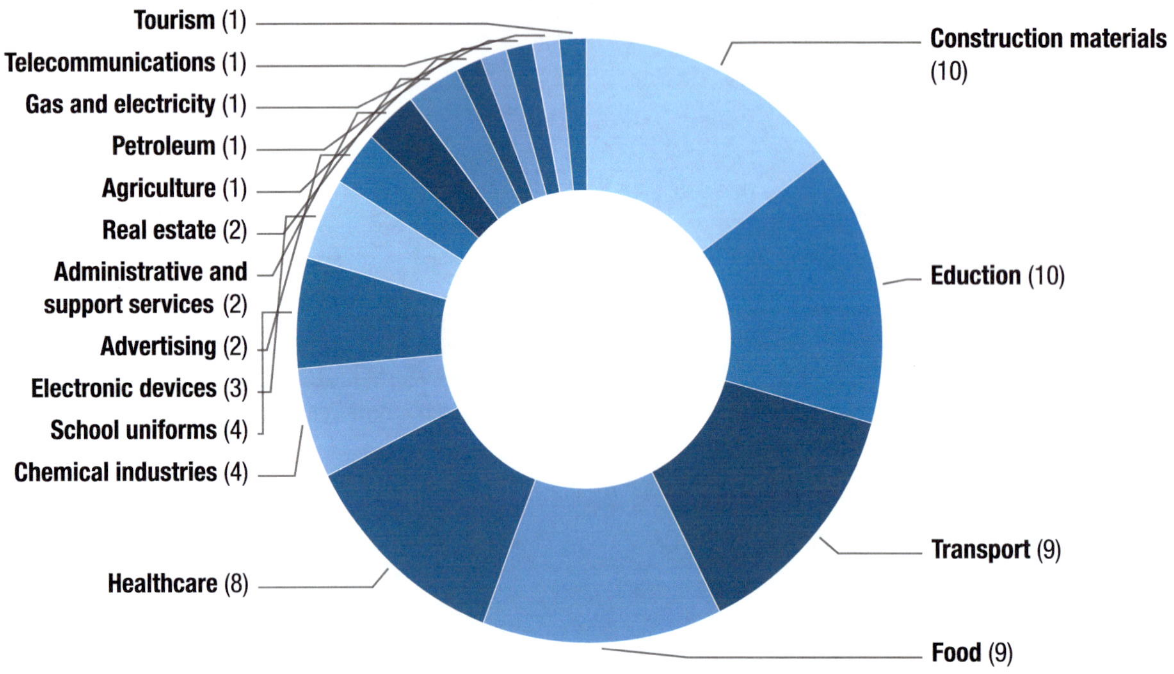

Accordingly, it can be observed that ECA has recently increased its enforcement efforts. This could be attributed to a number of factors, including possibly:

(1) ECA's increased role in the healthcare sector, due to its cooperation with the healthcare authorities for the purpose of reviewing transactions in the healthcare sector (see Section 2.1.4).

(2) A higher number of complaints and initiations, as evidenced by Figures 4 and 7. The increase in complaints could perhaps be due to a rising popularity of the authority, especially after the support received from the government regarding efforts in competitive neutrality.

(3) Increased and concentrated focus on enforcement, following its inclusion as a pillar in the 2021-2025 Strategy.

This underscores the need for more budgetary and human resources. Furthermore, these efforts can be supported by the publication of more guidelines, especially for SMEs, market players in informal sectors, as well as for business associations, along with increased media presence.

3.3. The role of private enforcement

Private enforcement is often seen as complementary to public enforcement, as well as a mechanism to guarantee the compensation of victims of anti-competitive practices.[187] Jurisdictions with private enforcement regimes for competition law often highlight the importance of streamlining both paths to achieving a more effective enforcement against anti-competitive

[187] See I. Lianos, P. Davis & P. Nebbia, Damages Claims for the Infringement of EU Competition Law, Oxford University Press, 2015.

practices. For instance, the European Union's Directive on certain rules governing actions for damages under national law for infringements of the competition law provisions of the member States and of the European Union describes the two systems stating that "both tools are required to interact to ensure maximum effectiveness of the competition rules".[188] These actions for damages can be following infringement decisions by the competition authority (follow-on actions) or relate to actions for damages brought directly against possible competition law infringements in civil courts (standalone actions).

The Egyptian legal system also allows for victims of anti-competitive practices to bring private civil claims against infringers using Article 163 of the Civil Code, which states that "[e]very fault which causes injury to another, imposes an obligation to make reparation upon the person by whom it is committed."

The extent to which ECA, or its decisions, are involved or referred to in civil proceedings can be described as arbitrary; there is no official policy or guidance on the matter. Data obtained from ECA shows that in at least three cases, one in 2015 and two in 2021, undertakings and individuals harmed by anti-competitive practices initiated private claims and referred to the respective infringement decisions issued by ECA. The 2015 case specifically offered interesting insights into the legal mechanisms at play, for instance setting out that once criminal proceedings are initiated, i.e. proceedings by the public prosecution following a request from ECA, the prescription period of the civil claim is paused until the final verdict is issued.[189] The court also referred to Article 163 of the Civil Code, quoted above, to state that damages may be granted even if a criminal conviction is not found. Indeed, while ECA's report was referred to during the proceedings and in the sentencing, it was not considered binding by civil courts.[190]

Moreover, it appears from documents provided by ECA that there are also at least three cases in which private damages were sought in standalone and not follow-on cases, namely in 2014, 2015, and 2018. These examples show the importance of streamlining the two enforcement mechanisms and issuing formal guidance from ECA, perhaps in cooperation with the judiciary, on the procedures of bringing a civil case to the courts, as well as outlining the role of ECA in the matter. Eventually, a registry of private actions for damages, or other private enforcement proceedings, could be compiled by ECA, in particular if legislation imposes the obligation to civil courts dealing with such cases to notify these actions for damages to ECA. This is particularly important for standalone cases, in order to provide ECA the possibility to present amicus curiae observations and engage with the analysis of the specific restrictions if this may prove helpful for the courts and the uniform application of ECL.[191]

[188] Directive 2014/104/EU of The European Parliament and of the Council of 26 November 2014 on certain rules governing actions for damages under national law for infringements of the competition law provisions of the member States and of the European Union, 2014, paragraph 6.

[189] Mohamed ElFar, Successful private damages case in Egypt: Case5/2013 Hewala Factory v Egyptian Co for Float Glass Judgment April 19, 2015 3rd Circuit, Civil Economic Appeals Mansoura Egypt (2015) 36(10) European Competition Law Review, p. 448 and 449 (note).

[190] Ibid, p. 450.

[191] Pursuant to Article 15(3) of Regulation 1/2003, the European Commission, acting on its own initiative, may submit written observations ("amicus curiae" observations) to courts of the member States where the coherent application of Article 101 or 102 of TFEU so requires.

Chapter IV

Recommendations

UN Trade and Development (UNCTAD) voluntary peer review of competition law and policy of Egypt recommends, among others: 1) substantial amendments and updates to the provisions in ECL and ECLER; 2) ECA is advised to publish merger guidelines and soft laws, given its sole jurisdiction over all competition matters in all sectors, and to cooperate in a more formal manner with Central Bank of Egypt and Financial Regulatory Authority; and 3) ECL and ECA need to be revised to give ECA overall more authority and independence to enhance efficiency and ensure more effective law enforcement. In this way, the legal and institutional frameworks for competition law in Egypt could be strengthened.

4. Recommendations

Following the above analysis, this Section sets out recommendations regarding the substance of ECL, issues of jurisdiction, and institutional design of the enforcement structures and practices of ECA. Most of the recommendations are made to the Egyptian government, as they concern changes to legislation. A summary of recommendations is included in Annex I.

4.1. Substance of Egyptian Competition Law

Recommendations to the government

1. The provisions in ECL and ECLER, relating to market definition and market power and analysing market power, namely Articles 3 and 4 of ECL and Articles 6 to 8 of ECLER have been used in relation to cases in the digital economy. However, the exhaustive nature of the definitions provided may not help their adaptability to the new realities of (digital) ecosystem competition and should be amended so as to enable the assessment of economic power and anti-competitive conduct in (digital) ecosystems.[192]

2. Article 6 of ECL currently lists four types of horizontal contracts/agreements which are prohibited without analysis of their anti-competitive effects. Paragraph 2 of Article 6 allows for an *ex-ante* exemption of such agreements, if ECA finds that it will result in economic efficiencies that outweigh the harm to competition and are passed on to the consumers. Article 7 of ECL prohibits all contracts/agreements between parties in a vertical relationship if they have a negative effect on competition, without setting a list of such practices.

   It is recommended that the two articles are merged into one provision dealing with all forms of collusive behaviour and all types of agreement (horizontal and vertical) that are prohibited *per se* unless exempted *ex-ante* by ECA, i.e. to include a list of the agreements that are anti-competitive *per se*.[193] Additionally, the concept of agreement or contract should be expanded to include concerted practices and decisions by associations of undertakings. Moreover, the mention of "relevant market" in relation to horizontal agreements should be removed to avoid confusion.

   Other types of horizontal and vertical agreements, for which ECA will need to prove at least potential anti-competitive effects, should be covered by Article 7 of ECL. For some of these categories of anti-competitive conduct (e.g. RPM), there would be a rebuttable presumption that they are capable of producing anti-competitive effects. This presumption may be rebutted by the parties if they manage to show that the specific conduct did not and/or cannot produce any anti-competitive effects. As such, the current structure of two separate provisions will be maintained with the following adjustments:

   (1) Article 6 of ECL would (a) state that it covers agreements and contracts, as well as concerted practices and decisions by an association of undertakings (with no mention of the "relevant market"), (b) provide an exhaustive list of *per se* restrictions of competition,

[192] An "ecosystem" may be defined as: (a) a nexus of interconnected and, to a great extent, interdependent economic activities of different undertakings aiming at the provision of products or services which impact on the same group of users; or (b) a platform connecting economic activities of different undertakings with the purpose of providing one or more products or services, affecting either the same users or different groups of business users or end users. See Ioannis Lianos, Reorienting Competition Law, Journal of Antitrust Enforcement, Volume 10, Issue 1, March 2022, p. 1-31.

[193] This could be the current list of agreements in Article 6 and some hardcore vertical restraints such as minimum RPM.

which should also include the exchange of commercially sensitive information and possibly minimum and fixed RPM wide MFN clauses, and restriction of passive sales leading to absolute territorial protection, and (c) provide the exemption mechanism currently laid out in Article 6(2) of ECL.

(2) Article 7 of ECL would (a) include a general provision or a list of prohibited horizontal or vertical agreements that may have a harmful effect on competition (those not listed in Article 6 of ECL), and if Article 6 of ECL is not modified to include vertical restraints, (b) layout explicitly that minimum and fixed RPM, wide MFN clauses, and restrictions of passive sales leading to absolute territorial protection are presumed to have a negative effect on competition, unless proven otherwise by the parties of the agreement (rebuttable presumption).

(3) Of particular interest could also be the development of specific class exemptions for small and medium firms in case they face asymmetrical bargaining power so as to be able to collectively bargain under certain circumstances without incurring the risk of infringing ECL.[194]

3. Article 8 of ECL provides an exhaustive list of prohibited practices, which does not include exploitative abuses, such as excessive pricing, and other conduct (exclusionary or exploitative) that might be relevant in the digital economy (e.g. excessive data extraction, self-preferencing, refusal to provide interoperability, data bundling). These practices should certainly be added to this list.[195] Conduct, such as margin squeeze and rebates, although arguably covered by Article 8(a) of ECL, should be added explicitly to increase legal certainty. In addition, regarding the establishment of a dominant position, it is recommended that Article 4 is amended to create a rebuttable presumption that undertakings with a market share of over 50 per cent are dominant in the relevant market, with no need to analyze the other two conditions for dominance (the ability to control prices and quantity independently of competitors). Accordingly, those with a market share of less than 25 per cent can be considered dominant, especially if they are found to enjoy a position of collective dominance with one or more other market players. The notion of collective dominance should be clarified explicitly in ECL. Eventually, Article 4 of ECL could be merged with Article 8 of ECL in order to address issues related to dominance within the same provision and avoid any confusions by the courts in the application of Article 4 of ECL in situations of abuse of dominance (and not for Article 6 purposes).[196]

4. Regarding the merger control regime, it is recommended that ECLER is updated in order to enact the regime as well as ensure legal certainty. Further, in order to comply with the COMESA Competition Regulations, ECA must remain the only point of contact for notifications referred to by the COMESA Competition Commission. This will help to prevent any procedural problems (e.g. fee division or meeting investigation deadlines) or substantive problems (e.g. the quality of assessment).

[194] The interview from the business association highlighted the difficulties faced by the millions of retailers and small local producers facing significant bargaining power in economically concentrated sectors. For an example of such class exemption for small and medium firms, see ACCC, Collective Bargaining Class Exemption (2021). Available at: https://www.accc.gov.au/public-registers/class-exemptions-register/collective-bargaining-class-exemption-0.

[195] The list of prohibited conduct if adopted by gatekeepers listed in Articles 5 and 6 of the Digital Markets Act (Regulation (EU) 2022/1925 of the European Parliament and of the Council of 14 September 2022 on contestable and fair markets in the digital sector and amending Directives (EU) 2019/1937 and (EU) 2020/1828, 2022 OJ L 265/1) may provide some examples of abusive conduct from which Article 8 of ECL may be inspired to expand its scope in the digital economy.

[196] This has happened in court decisions, including by the courts of appeal, in two cases: Mansoura Economic Court, Court of Appeal, Case No. 118 of 2019; and Mansoura Economic Court, Court of Appeal, Case No. 265 of 221.

Recommendations to ECA

5. Regarding anti-trust provisions, ECA may issue guidelines to enhance legal certainty and provide more clarity, for instance, concerning the application of Article 6 of ECL to information exchange and price signalling, as well as crisis cartels, and with regard to its enforcement practice concerning the interplay between Article 7 and Article 8 of ECL for vertical restraints.

6. Regarding the new merger control regime, it is recommended that ECA issue merger guidelines and soft laws clarifying its position on the substantive and procedural aspects relating to the regime, to ensure legal certainty. Its relationship with FRA should also be laid out clearly.

4.2. Jurisdiction to enforce competition law

Recommendations to the government

7. ECA should be given the sole jurisdiction over all competition matters in all sectors, including enforcement and merger control in the financial banking and non-banking sectors. This will ensure the consistent application of competition roles, the promotion of a more uniform competition law enforcement in all sectors, and the utilization of ECA's expertise in all sectors, thus achieving important economies of scale and learning effects in competition law enforcement. Furthermore, in order to comply with the COMESA Competition Regulations, ECA must remain the only point of contact for notifications referred to by the COMESA Competition Commission. This will help to prevent any procedural problems (like fee division or meeting investigation deadlines) or substantive problems (like the quality of assessment).

Recommendations to the government/CBE

8. It is recommended that the exemption of banking institutions from ECA's jurisdiction is abolished. This will lead to more consistent application of competition rules, lower risks of jurisdictional uncertainty, and lower risks of market players being able to exert influence on the sector regulator, given their close relationship.

   Alternatively, a mechanism of cooperation between ECA and CBE should be put in place, for instance, in the form of an MoU.

Recommendations to ECA/FRA

9. The powers of FRA regarding economic concentrations in the financial non-banking sector should be removed. Alternatively, members of ECA should be involved in the decision-making process in FRA and ECA and FRA should cooperate in a more formal manner. For instance, as FRA is the decision-making entity regarding such transactions, it should include members of ECA in its decision-making body when reaching a decision, in order to benefit from their expertise. This would ensure that ECA's non-binding opinions regarding mergers in the financial sector are thoroughly explained and accounted for in the FRA's decisions. This is increasingly important given the need to promote innovation in financial services and the emergence of fintech firms. An MoU between the two entities would help to clarify common issues.

4.3. Enforcement structures and practices of Egyptian Competition Authority

Recommendations to the government

10. It is recommended that the government consider an amendment to ECL, increasing the amount and providing more discretion to ECA as to setting the level of the fine and settlement amounts, eventually through the adoption of relevant guidelines. Moreover, whereas the current mechanism for setting fines and determining settlement amounts can cause practical difficulties in its application, it should be amended to account for the following:

Difficulty	Solution
It can be difficult to ascertain the duration of a violation/there is sometimes no duration for the violation.	Instead of calculating a portion of the revenue of the products subject to the violation for the duration of the violation, a percentage of the revenue should be derived from the financial year preceding the occurrence of the violation. Separately, or in addition to this amendment, a fee for simply entering into a hard-core agreement, even if it is of a short duration or not implemented, should be applied.[197]
It can be difficult to ascertain the products subject to the violation, or to separate their revenues from those derived by other products.	The revenues of all products affected directly or indirectly by the violation, which may sometimes include all products in the relevant market, should be the basis of the calculation.
In some cases - such as tying, bid-rigging or predatory pricing - the revenues of the products subject to the violation will not reflect the harm which occurred on the market.	Adjustments to the penalty should be allowed on a case-by-case basis, to be calculated in proportion to the exploitative or exclusionary harm caused, if it is possible to estimate. ECL should be amended to state that in cases where the fine or settlement amount, under the percentage option, would amount to EGP 0, the absolute value should be used.
ECA cannot settle with undertakings to an infringement unless all parties are willing to settle.	Hybrid settlements should be allowed in order to expedite procedures for undertakings willing to cooperate with ECA, as well as to avoid encouraging cartelists from colluding further. Undertakings that are not willing to settle would instead be referred to the public prosecution.

11. Furthermore, ECA does not currently have the power to issue administrative monetary/pecuniary sanctions. Other governmental authorities, such as CBE, have this power. Given ECA's experience in settlement procedures, which has increased in recent years, as evidenced by Table 3, and the extended duration of court proceedings as opposed to faster issuance of settlement decisions, ECL should be amended to provide ECA's Board with this power. Administrative monetary/pecuniary sanctions, as with any administrative decision, would be subject to judicial review by the State Council. It should also be possible to submit grievances regarding these decisions in front of an independent committee.

[197] See, for instance, Guidelines on the method of setting fines imposed pursuant to Article 23(2)(a) of Regulation No 1/2003, [2006] OJ C 210/2, paragraph 25, "[...] irrespective of the duration of the undertaking's participation in the infringement, the Commission will include in the basic amount a sum of between 15% and 25% of the value of sales [...] in order to deter undertakings from even entering into horizontal price-fixing, market-sharing and output-limitation agreements. The Commission may also apply such an additional amount in the case of other infringements. For the purpose of deciding the proportion of the value of sales to be considered in a given case, the Commission will have regard to a number of factors [...]".

This system would be employed in parallel to the criminal enforcement route, whereas the criminal route would prosecute individuals and the administrative route would sanction undertakings. This is especially important given the hurdles identified in Section 1.4.1 relating to the role of the public prosecution in bringing a case to court, whereas the public prosecution may choose to drop a case following its own investigation.

12. In addition, during court proceedings, ECA should be involved and be able to intervene as *amicus curiae*.[198] The same possibility for ECA to intervene as amicus curiae should also be provided for cases in civil courts.
13. A provision should also be added, prohibiting non-compliance with ECA's decisions and setting a fine (preferably administrative, to be issued by ECA) for such conduct.
14. Judges of the Economic Court should receive specialized training in competition law and economics matters. Competition law related cases should be allocated to a small pool of judges of the Economic Court, in order to retain expertise.
15. It is also recommended that alternative penalties are considered. This should be done with the aim of promoting deterrence, but without unduly reducing the number of capable businesses on the market. Suggestions include employing a mechanism to publish the names of directors involved in anti-competitive behaviour or eventually creating a compliance rating system for undertakings.
16. It is also recommended that ECA is given the power to impose hybrid settlements.
17. The decisions of ECA's Board should be given executive power, in order to grant ECA's administrative decisions more authority.
18. In addition, regarding investigation powers, it is recommended that an amendment to ECL is made to make it mandatory for persons who receive formal request for attendance from ECA to respond to these requests and/or participate in meetings with ECA. A sanction should also be added in a similar fashion to that of failure to cooperate in dawn raids or in providing information.
19. Further, on competitive neutrality, it is recommended that ECA's opinions regarding anti-competitive state measures are made binding on state entities, given the increased importance of maintaining competitive neutrality. Accordingly, state agencies that do not abide by ECA's written opinion would have to justify divergence.
20. It is also recommended that ECA's powers regarding market monitoring are increased; ECA should be given the power to issue behavioural and/or structural remedies following a market enquiry, subject to judicial review by the State Council.
21. Finally, it is recommended that ECA's financial resources, namely those allocated by the government, are increased and stable. One way to ensure that ECA's resources are proportional to the number of investigations it may/ought to carry out is by tying the budget

[198] Pursuant to Article 15(3) of Regulation 1/2003, the European Commission, acting on its own initiative, may submit written observations ("amicus curiae" observations) to courts of the member States where the coherent application of Article 101 or 102 of TFEU so requires.

to a fixed percentage of GDP.[199] This will allow ECA to hire more staff, on par with other competition authorities, including those in the region, and thus conclude more cases more efficiently. It is also recommended that the maximum wage for the employees of ECA is removed, in order to allow it to attract additional qualified candidates.

Recommendations to ECA

22. ECA should establish a prioritization mechanism for cases in order to deal with them in an efficient manner saving resources.

23. ECA should issue more guidelines, especially for SMEs, market players in informal sectors, as well as for business associations, in order to increase awareness of ECL.

24. ECA should also clarify the substantial basis and the procedures of private enforcement, in order to promote it as a tool complementary to public enforcement, eventually issuing documentation and reports to assist civil courts in assessing causality between the anti-competitive conduct and the damage and compute/estimate damages.

4.4. Enhancing the independence of Egyptian Competition Authority

Recommendations to the government

25. ECA should be granted a greater degree of independence, in line with Articles 215 and 216 of the Egyptian Constitution. This would grant ECA greater power as an institution, leading it, as the other supervisory authorities mentioned in Articles 215 and 216 of the Constitution, to be affiliated with the Head of the State, rather than the Prime Minister. It would also grant its employees the degree of impartiality and independence mentioned in Article 216 of the Constitution. Increased independence is particularly important in the context of reviewing anti-competitive state measures and promoting competitive neutrality; it would grant greater legal certainty, especially to investors, regarding the seriousness of the Competitive Neutrality Strategy. Moreover, it would eliminate any potential conflict of interest which may appear to occur in the review of anti-competitive state measures by any of the Ministerial Departments. Of course, care should be taken in the implementation of this system to guarantee the independence of ECA from any political interference.

26. Furthermore, the composition of ECA's Board should be amended to remove representatives from the government and the business community, in order to remove any political or commercial influence on decisions. The number of legal and economic experts on the Board should instead be increased.

[199] See, for instance, Greek Law 3959/2011 as amended in 2022, which provides in Article 17(1) that "(t)he revenue of the Competition Commission for the years 2021 and 2022 must at least amount to 0.0000368 of the Gross Domestic Product (GDP) of the financial year 2019, as set by the Hellenic Statistical Authority ("minimum revenue threshold"). For the years 2023 onwards the revenue of the Competition Commission must at least amount to 0.00004 (four of a billion) of the Gross Domestic Product (GDP) of the preceding financial year, as defined annually by the Hellenic Statistical Authority ("minimum revenue threshold"). If the Competition Commission revenue from the fees as set in the previous sub-section is lower than the minimum revenue threshold, the relevant amount shall be supplemented by the State budget following a decision of the Minister of Finance, which will be issued following a relevant request by the President of the Competition Commission. A decision of the Minister of Finance, following a request by the President of the Competition Commission, may increase the revenue of the Competition Commission through the State budget by a minimum of 0.00001 (one of a billion) of the Gross Domestic Product (GDP) of the preceding year, as set by the Hellenic Statistical Authority, provided that the Council of Experts of the Competition Commission referred to in paragraphs 3 and 4 of Article 22, holds, by a simple majority, that the medium-term objectives of the Competition Commission, based on its key performance indicators, have been achieved. This sum shall increase the Competition Commission revenue in the next financial year".

Annex I
Summary of recommendations

	Recommendation	Justification	Impact
		Substance of ECL	
For the government	Articles 3 and 4 of ECL and Articles 6 to 8 of ECLER, on market definition and market power, are amended.	The exhaustive nature of these articles makes them difficult to apply in markets where digital ecosystems may be present. These articles should therefore be amended to also enable the assessment of economic power and anticompetitive conduct in (digital) ecosystems. By adapting competition law to ecosystem competition and ecosystem power, there will be less need for adopting a regime of *ex-ante* regulation for digital platforms.	(1) Efficiency and clarity for ECA in defining the market in cases in the digital sector. (2) More effective competition law enforcement regarding market players in the digital sector.
	Article 6 is amended to include all (horizontal and vertical) *per se* prohibited conduct.	This will differentiate between per se and by-effect agreements, while allowing the exemption in Article 6(2) to continue for the former.	(1) Greater clarity for ECA, courts, and market players. (2) Wider application of Article 6 and hence greater deterrence of cartel behaviour, which would benefit the economy overall. [200]
	The mention of the "relevant market" in Article 6, in relation to horizontal agreements, should be removed.	Market definition does not need to be carried out in relation to horizontal agreements, so the phrase should be removed to avoid confusion.	(1) Greater clarity for ECA and courts. (2) More effective use of resources for ECA (as there will certainly be no need to define in-depth the market in cartel cases).

[200] Cartel behaviour can have an effect on multiple aspects of the economy, including labour. A study of anti-cartel legislation in the United Kingdom showed that cartels can lead to 20 to 30 per cent lower labour productive growth. See George Symeonidis, The Effect of Competition on Wages and Productivity: Evidence from the United Kingdom, 90, The Review of Economics and Statistics 1, 2008, p. 134-146. Available at: https://econpapers.repec.org/article/tprrestat/v_3a90_3ay_3a2008_3ai_3a1_3ap_3a134-146.htm.

Recommendation	Justification	Impact
Horizontal agreements/contracts, in Article 6, are expanded to include concerted practices and decisions by associations of undertakings. A class of exemptions may be added for small and medium firms in case they face asymmetrical bargaining power so as to be able to collectively bargain under certain circumstances without incurring the risk of infringing the ECL.	The concept needs to be expanded in order to more readily cover decisions taking place in industry chambers or by algorithms in digital markets.	(1) Greater clarity for ECA, courts, and market players. (2) More effective competition law enforcement
Article 7 is amended to explicitly list all (horizontal and vertical) by-effect conduct (i.e. other types of agreements for which ECA will need to prove actual or potential anticompetitive effects), not listed in Article 6.	The current form of Article 7 is difficult to apply, as it does not provide guidance on what may be considered anti-competitive vertical restraints.	(1) Greater clarity for ECA, courts, and market players. (2) More effective competition law enforcement
Article 7 is amended to place a rebuttable presumption that minimum and fixed RPM, wide MFN clauses, and restrictions of passive sales leading to absolute territorial protection are presumed to be capable of producing anti-competitive effects (whereas pro-competitive effects would be put forward by the parties to the agreement).	This conduct should be differentiated from other by-effect conduct, as it is more likely to harm competition.	(1) Greater power to pursue these cases, with less resources needed. (2) Increased deterrence leading to more effective competition law enforcement
Article 8 is amended to include exploitative abuses, such as excessive pricing, and other conduct (exclusionary or exploitative) that might be relevant in the digital economy (e.g. excessive data extraction, self-preferencing, refusal to provide interoperability, data bundling).	This conduct is currently not covered by Article 8 ECL.	(1) Enhanced capacity to intervene against exploitative conduct in key sectors (e.g. pharmaceuticals) and anti-competitive conduct in digital markets.
Margin squeeze and rebates should be added explicitly to Article 8.	This conduct may be covered by Article 8(a), but this is unclear and it reduces legal certainty.	(1) Greater clarity for ECA, courts, and market players.

	Recommendation	Justification	Impact
	Article 4 is amended to create a rebuttable presumption that undertakings with a market share of over 50 per cent are dominant in the relevant market, with no need to analyse the other two conditions for dominance (the ability to control prices and quantity independently of competitors). Accordingly, those with a market share of less than 25 per cent could be considered dominant, especially if they are found to enjoy a position of collective dominance with one or more other market players. Eventually, Article 4 could be merged with Article 8 in order to address issues related to dominance within the same provision and avoid any confusion by the courts in the application of Article 4 in situations of abuse of dominance (and not for Article 6 purposes).	Market players with a market share of over 50 per cent are likely to be dominant, so reducing the burden of having to prove further criteria will save on ECA's resources. Having a rebuttable presumption means that the parties can refute this claim. Additionally, the notion of collective dominance should be clarified in ECL, given the situation of an oligopoly in which there may be a high likelihood of coordinated or non-coordinated effects, even if each of the undertakings involved has on its own less than 25 per cent market share.	(1) Greater clarity for ECA, courts, and market players. (2) More effective use of resources for ECA.
	Regarding the new merger control regime, ECLER should be updated in order to enact the regime as well as ensure legal certainty.	The ECLER is yet to be updated, more than a year after the amendment of ECL.	(1) Greater clarity for ECA, courts, and market players.
	ECA remains the only point of contact for merger notifications referred to by the COMESA Competition Commission.	ECA has successfully assessed more than 150 cases referred by the COMESA Competition Commission since 2015. This cooperation between ECA and the COMESA Competition Commission should continue vis-à-vis all economic sectors.	(1) Prevention of any procedural problems (e.g. fee division or meeting investigation deadlines) or substantive problems (e.g. the quality of assessment).
For ECA	ECA issues more guidelines to provide more clarity, for instance, concerning the application of Article 6 to information exchange and price signalling, as well as crisis cartels, and with regard to enforcement practice concerning the interplay between Article 7 and Article 8 for vertical restraints.	These issues are not clear in the law and should be clarified by ECA in the absence of decisional practice.	(1) Greater clarity for ECA, courts, and market players.

	Recommendation	Justification	Impact
	ECA issues merger guidelines and soft laws clarifying its position on the substantive and procedural aspects relating to the regime. Its relationship with FRA should also be laid out clearly.	Detailed guidance will need to be provided for this novel area of the law.	(1) Greater clarity for ECA, courts, and market players. (2) Will improve legal certainty for economic concentrations.
	Jurisdiction to enforce competition law		
For the government	ECA is given exclusive jurisdiction to enforce competition law across all sectors.	Banks are currently exempt from ECL, and FRA receives notifications and issues final decisions regarding economic concentrations in the financial non-banking sector.	(1) Consistent application of competition law. (2) Coherent, state-wide competition policy. (3) Utilization of ECA's expertise.
For the government/CBE	The exemption for banking institutions from ECA's jurisdiction is abolished.	Banks are currently exempt from ECL, and are instead under the jurisdiction of CBE for competition matters.	(1) More consistent application of competition rules. (2) Lower risks of jurisdictional uncertainty, and lower risks of market players being able to exert influence on the sector regulator, given their close relationship.
For ECA/FRA	The special system for economic concentrations in the financial non-banking sector should be removed. Alternatively, ECA and FRA should cooperate in a more formal manner and members of ECA should be involved in the decision-making process in FRA regarding these economic concentrations.	Consistency in the merger control regime, including for transactions in the financial non-banking sector, must be established.	(1) More consistent application of competition rules. (2) Ensures that FRA benefits from ECA's expertise. (3) More effective competition-enhancing regulation of the financial sector and fintech companies.
	Enforcement structures and practices of ECA		
For the government	Fine and settlement amounts for infringements of ECL are increased.	The last amendments to the fine and settlement amounts took place in 2014, before multiple factors impacted the inflation and the value of EGP.	(1) Increased deterrence.
For the government	ECA is given the power to impose hybrid settlements (where some undertakings settle with ECA and the rest are referred to the public prosecution).	ECA currently cannot accept a request for settlement, unless submitted by all parties to the violation. This can discourage undertakings from settling with ECA, as well as encourage colluding firms to continue to cooperate.	(1) Easier settlement procedures, leading to expedited closing of cases, administrative procedure economies and hence enhanced deterrence.

Recommendation	Justification	Impact
Fines should be calculated as a percentage of the revenue of the financial year preceding the occurrence of the violation. A fee for simply entering a hard-core agreement, even if it is of a short duration or not implemented, should be applied.	Currently, in calculating fine and settlement amounts, it can be difficult to ascertain the duration of a violation/there is sometimes no duration for the violation.	(1) Greater clarity for ECA, courts, and market players.
The revenues of all products effected directly or indirectly by the violation, which may sometimes include all products in the relevant market, should be the basis of the calculation of the fine or settlement.	Currently, it can be difficult to ascertain the products subject to the violation, or to separate their revenues from those derived by other products.	(1) Greater clarity for ECA, courts, and market players.
In cases - such as tying, bid-rigging or predatory pricing - where the revenues of the products subject to the violation do not reflect the harm which occurred on the market, adjustments to the penalty should be allowed on a case-by-case basis, to be calculated in proportion to the exploitative or exclusionary harm caused if it is possible to estimate. ECL should also be amended to state that in cases where the fine or settlement amount, under the percentage option, would amount to EGP 0, the absolute value should be used.	In such cases, calculating the fine based on a percentage of revenue may not be reflective of the harm caused to the market.	(1) Increased deterrence.
ECA's board is given the power to issue administrative monetary/ pecuniary sanctions. An independent committee is created in ECA to review grievances of such decisions.	Sanctions can currently only be issued by the courts. Court decisions can take many years. A decision may not reach the court if it is turned down by the public prosecution. Judges and public prosecutors may not be experienced in competition law.	(1) Expedited fining procedures. (2) Increased deterrence. (3) More specialized decision-making. (4) Accountability is maintained through the independent committees and through the existing system of appeal before the State Council.
ECA is given the power to request a case is filed in court, in addition to the power to refer a case to the public prosecution.	ECA currently only has the power to refer cases to the public prosecution, reducing its involvement in proceedings after the reference is made.	(1) Greater involvement of ECA post-referral, which would benefit the prosecution from ECA's expertise, and ECA from the prosecution's investigative powers.

	Recommendation	Justification	Impact
	ECA is involved in court proceedings and is able to intervene as amicus curiae (including in civil courts). Judges of the Economic Courts should receive specialized training in competition law and economic matters. Competition law related cases should be allocated to a small pool of judges of the Economic Courts, in order to retain expertise.	Economic Courts, while generally specialized in economic and financial matters, may not be specifically specialized in competition law. Involving ECA in court proceedings will cover this gap. Additionally, an important effort should be made to train the judges of the Economic Courts in competition law and economics.	(1) More specialized decision making. (2) More training for the judges of the Economic Courts in competition law and economics and creation of a pool of highly specialized judges at the Economic Courts to hear competition cases.
	An article is added to ECL prohibiting non-compliance with ECA's decisions and setting a fine (preferably administrative, to be issued by ECA) for this conduct.	There is currently no such article in ECL, reducing from the power of ECA's administrative decisions.	(1) Increased deterrence.
	The following alternatives penalties should be considered: director disqualification, naming-and-shaming of individuals involved in anti-competitive behaviour, and/or eventually creating a compliance rating system for undertakings.	As the law is criminal in nature, it prosecutes individuals. Individual deterrence should accordingly be increased through these non-pecuniary sanctions.	(1) Increased deterrence.

Recommendation	Justification	Impact
ECA is granted the degree of independence stipulated in Articles 215 and 216 of the Egyptian Constitution.	This would provide ECA similar degree of independence as other supervisory authorities mentioned in Articles 215 and 216 of the Constitution. It would also grant its employees the degree of impartiality and independence mentioned in Article 216 of the Constitution. Increased independence is particularly important in the context of reviewing anti-competitive state measures and promoting competitive neutrality; it would grant greater legal certainty, especially to investors, regarding the seriousness of the Competitive Neutrality Strategy. Moreover, association with the President rather than the Prime Minister would also eliminate any potential conflict of interest which may appear to occur in the review of anti-competitive state measures by any of the Ministries. Of course, care should be taken in the implementation of this system to guarantee the independence of ECA from any political interference.	(1) Enhanced role and resources for ECA, ultimately leading to increased deterrence. (2) Legal certainty for investors regarding serious efforts to implement the Competitive Neutrality Strategy and create a level playing field. (3) Increased economic growth and productivity, as well as lower prices, due to the lessening of anti-competitive state measures.[201]
Article 12 of ECL is amended to remove representation in ECA's Board from the government (i.e. from ministries) or from the business community. Instead, the number of experts is increased.	ECA's Board should mainly be comprised of legal and economic experts, in order to ensure enhanced impartiality and to improve the accuracy of its decisions.	(1) Ensures the impartiality of the Board.

[201] Jens Arnold et al., Regulation, Resource Reallocation and Productivity Growth, 16 European Investment Bank Papers 1, 2011, p. 90-115. Available at: http://www.eib.org/attachments/efs/eibpapers/eibpapers_2011_v16_n01_en.pdf#page=92; and Guglielmo Barone and Federico Cingano, Service Regulation and Growth: Evidence from OECD Countries, Bank of Italy Temi di Discussione (Working Paper) No. 675, 2008. Available at: http://papers.ssrn.com/sol3/papers.cfm?abstract_id=1160183.

Recommendation	Justification	Impact
The decisions of ECA's Board should be given executive power.	(1) The fact that ECA's decisions would have "executive power" would help ECA promote the rapid enforcement and execution of its decisions. This would be particularly helpful in cases in the digital market where market changes occur rapidly, which requires quick execution of the decision. (2) In all cases, ECA's decisions would be subject to judicial review.	(1) More efficient use of resources. (2) Faster intervention in cases in dynamic markets, such as digital markets.
ECL amended to make it mandatory for persons who receive formal requests for attendance from ECA to respond to these requests and/or participate in meetings with ECA, otherwise they would face a fine.	ECA does not currently have this power, possibly impeding it from carrying out stakeholder interviews efficiently.	(1) Enhanced efficiency in conducting investigations.
ECA's opinions regarding anti-competitive state measures are made binding on state entities. Entities that do not abide by ECA's opinion must justify this in writing.	While entities are bound to consult ECA on state measures related to competition, they are not currently bound by ECA's decision.	(1) Enhanced competitive neutrality. (2) Expedited decision making regarding competitive neutrality. (3) Empowers citizens to make claims at administrative courts if they are harmed by anti-competitive state measures.
ECA is given the power to issue behavioural and/or structural remedies following a market enquiry, subject to judicial review by the State Council.	ECA can only currently use market enquiries to uncover violations to ECL or to issue recommendations regarding legislation, in line with Article 11/5 ECL.	(1) More effective ex-ante prevention of anti-competitive practices. (2) More efficient use of market monitoring powers.
ECA's budget is increased and made more stable by tying it to a fixed percentage of GDP.	ECA's budget is lower than global averages, keeping it from being able to hire more staff. This is especially necessary given ECA's increased workload in recent years.	(1) Enhanced and more efficient enforcement. (2) Studies show a relationship between economic growth and competition policy funding; a multi-jurisdictional study has shown economic growth increase by 0.84 per cent.[202]
The maximum wage for the employees of ECA is removed.	This will allow ECA to attract an increased number of qualified candidates.	(1) Enhanced and more efficient enforcement.

[202] Joseph A Claugherty, Competition Policy Trends and Economic Growth: Cross-National Empirical Evidence, 17 International Journal of the Economics of Business, 1, 2010, p. 111-127. Available at: https://www.tandfonline.com/doi/abs/10.1080/13571510903516995#.U75kIPmSyVM.

	Recommendation	Justification	Impact
For ECA	ECA establishes a prioritization mechanism for cases in order to deal with them in an efficient manner that saves resources.	ECA does not currently employ such a methodology.	(1) Enhanced and more efficient enforcement.
	ECA issues guidance on compliance for SMEs, market players in informal sectors, as well as for business associations.	While more guidelines have recently been published by ECA, further guidance will ensure greater awareness by different players in the business community.	(1) Enhanced and more efficient enforcement. (2) Increased awareness of ECA's role and powers.
	ECA issues guidance on the substantial basis and the procedures of private enforcement.	While private claims are possible, they are sometimes removed from the existing competition expertise, weakening their potentially positive effect on enforcement.	(1) Enhanced and more efficient enforcement.

	Recommendation	Justification	Impact
	Enhancing the Independence of ECA		
For the government	ECA is granted the degree of independence stipulated in Articles 215 and 216 of the Egyptian Constitution.	This would provide ECA a similar degree of independence as other supervisory authorities mentioned in Articles 215 and 216 of the Constitution. It would also grant its employees the degree of impartiality and independence mentioned in Article 216 of the Constitution. Increased independence is particularly important in the context of reviewing anti-competitive state measures and promoting competitive neutrality; it would grant greater legal certainty, especially to investors, regarding the seriousness of the Competitive Neutrality Strategy. Moreover, association with the President rather than the Prime Minister would also eliminate any potential conflict of interest which may appear to occur in the review of anti-competitive state measures by any of the Ministries. Of course, care should be taken in the implementation of this system to guarantee the independence of ECA from any political interference.	(1) Enhanced role and resources for ECA, ultimately leading to increased deterrence. (2) Legal certainty for investors regarding serious efforts to implement the Competitive Neutrality Strategy and create a level playing field. (1) Increased economic growth and productivity, as well as lower prices, due to the lessening of anti-competitive state measures.
	Article 12 of ECL is amended to remove representation in ECA's Board from the government (i.e. from ministries) or from the business community. Instead, the number of experts is increased.	ECA's Board should mainly be comprised of legal and economic experts, in order to ensure enhanced impartiality and to improve the accuracy of its decisions.	(1) Ensures the impartiality of the Board.

Annex II
Evolution of Egyptian Competition Law

ECL was promulgated on 15 February 2005. Article 4 of its preamble stated that it would be enacted 3 months later, on 16 May 2005. It came into force with the enactment of ECLER on 18 August 2005,[203] and subsequently the appointment of ECA's Board of Directors on 24 August 2005.[204] This was followed by the hiring of technical staff, which took place from that date until early 2006.[205]

ECL and ECLER were amended, as of the drafting of this Report, on the following dates:

Table 4
Summary of Amendments to ECL and ECLER

Date of ECL amendment	Law No.	Date of corresponding ECLER amendment	Decision No.
22 June 2008, enacted on 23 June 2008	Law No. 190 of 2008 and Law No. 193 of 2008	13 November 2010, enacted on 14 November 2010	Prime Ministerial Decision No. 2957 of 2010
02 July 2014, enacted on 03 July 2014	Law No. 56 of 2014	20 September 2016, enacted on 21 September 2016	Prime Ministerial Decision No. 2509 of 2016
08 April 2019, enacted on 09 April 2019	Law No. 15 of 2019	No amendment required	
29 December 2022, enacted on 30 December 2022	Law No. 175 of 2022	Amendment not yet issued as of the date of the drafting this Report	

The remainder of this Section will primarily focus on laying out the content of ECL and ECLER, explaining the amendments throughout, with a focus on the substantive aspects of the law as well as the provisions relating to procedures and to ECA as an institution.

A1.1. The original version of Egyptian Competition Law and Egyptian Competition Law Executive Regulations

The original text of ECL was first issued within the political and economic context described in Section 1.2.

The general aim of the Egyptian competition policy is laid out in Article 1: that economic activity is carried out in a manner that does not prevent, restrict, or harm competition, in line with the provisions of ECL. The text then proceeds to cover the substantive elements, or the main

[203] The Executive Regulations were issued via Prime Ministerial Decision No. 1316 of 2005 on 16 August 2005. They were published in the Official Gazette on 17 August 2005, to be enacted the next day.
[204] Egypt, Prime Ministerial Decision No. 1342 of 2005.
[205] ECA's Annual Report 2006-07. Available (in Arabic) at: https://eca.org.eg/getattachment/9b7a1346-d222-4513-aae2-d9ea38c5b10e/%D8%A7%D9%84%D8%AA%D9%82%D8%B1%D9%8A%D8%B1-%D8%A7%D9%84%D8%B3%D9%86%D9%88%D9%8A-%D9%84%D8%B9%D8%A7%D9%85%D9%8A-2006-2007.pdf.

prohibitions: horizontal agreements, vertical agreements, and abuse of dominant position.

Article 6 of ECL provides an exhaustive list of prohibited horizontal contracts or agreements, namely those which may result in:

(1) Increasing, decreasing, or setting prices.

(2) Market allocation.

(3) Coordination in relation to procurement (bid-rigging).

(4) Limiting the manufacturing, distribution, or marketing of a product.

The article, in its opening sentence, refers to the relevant market, by which Article 3 of ECL clarifies the product and geographic market. Combined with the text of Article 6 of ECLER, it is evident that the test for defining the product market is two-fold, and that it is done from the point of view of the consumer:

(1) Products in the same market are those that are similar in terms of usage and characteristics.

(2) Consumers must be able to switch between products.

As for the geographic market, Article 3 of ECL and Article 6 of ECLER clarify that it is the area in which competition conditions are homogenous.

The concept of competitor(s) is defined in Article 11 of ECLER as "those working in the same relevant market at present or those capable of working in it in the future [...]", thus including potential competitors.

Article 7 of ECL prohibits any agreement or contract between a person and anyone they have an upstream or downstream relationship with if it may result in limiting competition. The article does not lay out a list of such agreements.

Article 8 of ECL addresses the abuse of a dominant position. Similar to Article 6 of ECL, it lays out an exhaustive list of prohibited practices, which include exclusivity, tying and bundling, discrimination, and predatory pricing. The text of the article states that such practices are prohibited for a person who occupies a dominant position in a relevant market; the criteria for determining the relevant market being described in Article 3 of ECL. Article 4 of ECL and Articles 7 and 8 of ECLER are relevant for assessing dominance. Read together, they clarify that for an undertaking to be dominant, it must hold a 25 per cent share of the relevant market, as well as having the ability to control prices and quantity. The latter is decided with reference to a number of factors, such as: previous behaviour of the incumbent, the number of competitors and their relative market shares, ease of access to the material and distribution channels necessary to operate on the market, and barriers to entry and expansion.

Other key aspects laid out in the original version of the law included:

(1) Article 5 of ECL, which clarifies that ECL applies to conduct that takes place outside of Egypt if it results in preventing, restricting, or harming the freedom of competition in Egypt.

(2) Article 9 of ECL, which lays out that public utilities managed by the state are exempt from ECL. At the time, those that were managed by private players could also apply for an exemption from the prohibitions laid out in Articles 6 to 8 of ECL, if the action in question resulted in a public benefit that outweighed the harm on competition and was passed on to consumers.

(3) Article 10 of ECL, which allows the Cabinet of Ministers to set prices for strategic goods for a limited period of time, after consulting ECA.

The remainder of the law sets out procedural rules and the institutional design. For instance, Article 11 of ECL lays out the role of ECA, explaining that it is mainly to: receive complaints (from natural and juristic persons), receive requests from state bodies to launch investigations, as well as initiate investigations, create a database of economic activity in Egypt, issue opinions regarding state measures, and coordinate with sectoral regulators on joint issues. It also clarifies that ECA is affiliated with the "competent minister". Article 2 of the law's preamble clarifies that the competent minister is the Prime Minister. Notably, however, these powers were delegated to the Minister of Trade and Industry shortly after ECA's creation.[206] The practical implications of this "affiliation" are discussed in Section 3.2.1.

Article 12 of ECL relates to the membership of ECA's Board, which at the time included: a chairperson appointed on a full-time basis, a judge, four representatives from different government ministries, three experts, and six individuals to represent the business community, the banking association, and the consumer association.

Also related to ECA's independence is Article 14 of ECL, on the sources of ECA's budget. According to this provision, ECA has an independent budget, which comprises a portion of the general state budget and varies each year,[207] any grants given to ECA (such as those from international organizations), if in line with its duties and if accepted by the Board with fees received from carrying out its duties under the law (through later amendments, as explained in this section, these currently include: merger notifications, applications under Article 6(2) of ECL, and applications under Article 9 of ECL,[208] as well as fees for obtaining official copies of documents that ECA is permitted to share[209]).

Finally, Articles 20 to 22 of ECL lay out ECA's decision-making powers, as well as the fine and settlement amounts. Article 20 of ECL explained that, upon uncovering an infringement of Articles 6 to 8, ECA's Board is to order the infringer(s) to cease the anti-competitive practice immediately or within a set period. For the matter to be pursued further, namely, by the public prosecution, a reference would have to be made by the competent minister (the Prime Minister, or the Minister of Trade and Industry in regard to the delegation granted at the time).[210] The relevant minister could also take the decision to settle with the infringer(s), for an amount between EGP 60,000 (US$ 1,277) and EGP 20,000,000 (US$ 425,758).[211] Fines issued from the court, however, ranged from EGP 30,000 (US$ 639) to EGP 10,000,000 (US$ 212,879), or any amount the court found to equate to the "value of the infringing product".[212]

As such, it is apparent that the original version of ECL included three main infringements, the possibility of an exemption in Article 9 of ECL, as well as a structure for the functioning of ECA and its Board. It did, however, lack any system relating to merger control.

A1.2. 2008: a merger notification regime and increased fines

In 2008, the law was amended to bring in a major substantive reform, as well as some procedural changes.

The major amendment was that of Article 19 of ECL. A paragraph was added to the article, making it mandatory for persons to notify ECA of the following: a merger between two or more persons; establishing a joint venture between two or more persons; and the acquisition of an asset, usufruct, rights of property or stocks, or combination of management between two or more persons, if the combined turnover of the persons surpassed EGP 100,000 (US$ 2,129).

[206] This delegation was repealed in August 2022 through Prime Ministerial Decision No. 2934 of 2022.This is discussed further in Section 3.2.1.
[207] See Section 3.2.6.
[208] See Annex A.1.3.
[209] Articles 29 and 30 of ECLER.
[210] Article 21 of ECL.
[211] Ibid.
[212] Article 22 of ECL.

Articles 44 and 45 of ECLER were added to provide more details on this system, detailing that notifications must be made 30 days after the transaction is implemented. It is clear from the text that this ex-post notification system was not a merger control regime *per se*, as ECA only had the power to receive notifications, but not to make decisions regarding the transactions notified. A fine for failure to notify, of between EGP 10,000 (US$ 213) to EGP 100,000 (US$ 2,129), was added as Article 22 bis of ECL. This article also added the same fine for failing to provide ECA with requested data, as well as a fine ranging between EGP 20,000 (US$ 426) to EGP 200,000 (US$ 4,258) for knowingly providing ECA with incorrect information.

In addition, the fine for violating Articles 6 to 8 of ECL was raised to range from EGP 100,000 (US$ 2,129) to EGP 300,000,000 (US$ 6,386,370). A paragraph was also added to Article 22 of ECL to double the amount of the fine in cases of repeated offenses (recidivism).

All in all, the major amendment in 2008 was that relating to the *ex-post* notification requirement for mergers.

In terms of ECA's enforcement record at the time, it is worth noting two important cases in the cement and steel sectors.

Box 5
Steel Investigation

In 2007, the Minister of Trade and Industry instructed ECA to launch an investigation in the steel sector. ECA finalized this investigation, which covered the period 2005-2007, and 2009. The investigation mainly concerned with the major undertaking in this sector, Ezzsteel, which at the time, was the largest company in Egypt.

The investigation concluded that Ezzsteel had a dominant position under ECL, but that it had not violated Article 7 nor Article 8 of ECL. While ECA did find an increase in the price of steel, it found that this was proportionate to the increasing costs of production as well as rising demand.

A second investigation, finalized in 2012, was launched covering the period 2007-2011, this time focusing on the vertical distributional aspects of Ezzsteel's conduct, again finding no violation by Ezzsteel. In that report, ECA did not find Ezzsteel to occupy a dominant position on the market, given the high volumes of imported steel, seemingly taking a different perspective than its finding in the previous investigation. ECA based this finding of lack of dominance on the argument that once the import of steel was facilitated in 2008, Ezzsteel could no longer be considered a dominant firm, despite holding 51 per cent share of local production (according to their report).

In 2011, the public prosecution decided to pursue a case against Ezzsteel, or specifically its founder, Ahmed Ezz, for violating ECL, irrespective of ECA's findings. Following acquittal by the first level court, the Court of Appeal found Ahmed Ezz, and other senior members of the company, guilty of a violation to Article 7 of ECL and issued the maximum fine at the time: 100 million EGP (2.1 million US$). The fine was later reduced to EGP 10 million (0.2 million US$), due to a legal principle that dictates that the fine applied should be the one stipulated in the law at the time the crime was committed.[213]

[213] Dina I Waked, Law, Society, and the Market: Living with Egypt's Competition Law 2005-2015, Law and Society in Post-Revolution Egypt (AUC Press), 2018, p. 14-19. Available at: https://papers.ssrn.com/sol3/papers.cfm?abstract_id=3091552.

Box 6
Cement Investigation

The Minister of Trade and Industry instructed ECA to carry out an investigation into the cement sector directly following the issue of ECL. The investigation covered the period between 2005 and 2007, and was finalized in 2007.[214]

ECA found a number of undertakings operating in the market for a commonly used type of cement to have agreed to limit production, given the fact that the price of cement had recently decreased. The agreement had taken place in 2003, before the enactment of ECL, and was rubber-stamped by the Ministry. The agreement continued to be implemented following the enactment of the law, and cement prices did in fact increase. As such, ECA found 9 undertakings to have infringed Article 6 clauses (a) and (d) of ECL. The Minister of Trade and Industry agreed with ECA's request to refer the case to the public prosecution.

The case was then referred to Economic court and became the first judicial finding of a violation of ECL. The court refuted the parties' arguments relating to lack of evidence of an agreement and the existence of economic justifications. The court issued the maximum fine at the time, EGP 10 million (US$ 0.2 million), for each director and chairman of the nine undertakings involved in the cartel. The decision was upheld by the Court of Appeal in December 2008.[215]

The 2014 amendments, as will be laid out in the following Section, brought further amendments to the law.

A1.3. 2014: major amendments

The 2014 amendments brought multiple changes to ECL.

Perhaps one of the key amendments was the limitation of the exemption regime laid out in Article 9 of ECL. The article was amended to allow for an exemption from Articles 6 to 8 of ECL only for public utilities managed directly by the state.[216] Public utilities managed indirectly by the state could apply for this exemption, and it would only be allowed by ECA if the practices served the public interest, or if they created benefits to consumers which outweigh the harm to competition. Notably, ECA has since only received one application for this exemption.[217]

[214] Dina I Waked, Law, Society, and the Market: Living with Egypt's Competition Law 2005-2015, Law and Society in Post-Revolution Egypt (AUC Press), 2018, p. 14-19. Available at: https://papers.ssrn.com/sol3/papers.cfm?abstract_id=3091552.

[215] Mohamed ElFar, Egypt - Case No 2900/2008 Felonies of Madinit Nasr Awal (25/08/2008); (Appeal No 22622/2008 East Cairo) Prosecution vs. Suez Cement Group, La Farge Titan Group, Al-Amreya Simpore Group, Simx Egypt (Assyout Cement), Egyptian Cement, Sinai Cement, Misr -- Bani Suef for Cement, National Cement Company - The First Court Decision under Egyptian Competition Law, 2 Global Antitrust Review ([2009]) 116 (note). Available at: http://www.icc.qmul.ac.uk/media/icc/gar/gar2009/GAR-On-line-El-Far-Case-Note-7.pdf.

[216] The concept of public utility is not defined in ECL or in other statutes, but it has been defined in a decision issued by the Administrative Court on 2 June 1957 as, "Any project created and managed by the state in a sustainable manner [...] and has a special characteristic in that it provides a public good, meaning that it aims provide a common need or provide a public service". Public utilities are managed by the state either directly or indirectly. The former describes a case in which the public utility is managed by the state using its own financial and human resources. However, indirect management entails that the public utility is managed by a private company, with the state being involved either as a partner of the company or by leasing it to the company for a share of the benefits or for a limited period.

[217] Data obtained from ECA.

Additionally, a second paragraph was added to Article 6 of ECL, allowing for parties to a horizontal agreement, which would otherwise infringe Article 6, to apply for an exemption before carrying out the agreement, on the basis that it generates economic efficiencies, which outweigh the harm on competition. Economic efficiencies are defined in Article 2(e) of ECL as, "The reduction of the average variable cost of producing goods, the enhancement of quality, or optimizing the volume of goods produced or its distribution or the production or distribution of novel goods or the acceleration of its production or distribution". The application would be reviewed by ECA and would be granted, according to Article 17 of ECLER, for a renewable period of two years.

In terms of ECA's advocacy powers, its mandate to provide an opinion regarding state measures was expanded through an amendment to Article 11 of ECL, making it mandatory for state authorities to consult ECA before issuing state measures that may have an effect on competition.

The composition of ECA's Board was also modified through amendments to Article 12 of ECL, which brought down the number of ministerial representatives to two rather than four previously and to three representatives of business and consumer associations,[218] instead of six previously.

The Board was granted the power through an amendment to Article 20 of ECL to issue decisions on interim measures in cases where it was apparent that otherwise, an irreversible harm to competition may materialize. Article 21 of ECL was also amended, granting the Board the power to refer cases to the public prosecution and to settle with infringers - a major change in contrast with the previous system in which only the relevant minister had his power.

In addition, the method of calculating fines and settlement amounts was changed into a system in which the fine or settlement amount would constitute a percentage of the revenue of the product(s) directly affected by the infringement, or an absolute value if this could not be calculated (for infringements of Articles 6 to 8 of ECL), varying accordingly to the nature of the infringement (horizontal or vertical agreement, abuse of dominant position, etc.), as follows:

[218] Namely, three members representing the General Federation of the Chambers of Commerce, the Egyptian Federation of Industries, and the General Federation for Consumer Protection.